Louisiana Bucket List Adventure Guide

*Explore 100 Offbeat
Destinations You Must Visit!*

Deborah Gibson

Canyon Press
canyon@purplelink.org

Please consider writing a review!
Just visit: purplelink.org/review

ISBN: 978-1-957590-10-3

FREE BONUS

Discover 31 Incredible Places You Can
Visit Next! Just Go To:

purplelink.org/travel

Table of Contents:

New Orleans

How to Use This Book

Welcome to your very own adventure guide to exploring the many wonders of the state of Louisiana. Not only does this book offer the most wonderful places to visit and sights to see in the vast state, but it provides GPS coordinates for Google Maps to make exploring that much easier.

Adventure Guide
Sorted by region, this guide offers over 100 amazing wonders found in Louisiana for you to see and explore. They can be visited in any order and this book will help you keep track of where you've been and where to look forward to going next. Each section describes the area or place, what to look for, how to get there, and what you may need to bring along.

GPS Coordinates
As you can imagine, not all of the locations in this book have a physical address. Fortunately, some of our listed wonders are either located within a National Park or Reserve, or near a city, town, or place of business. For those that are not associated with a specific location, it is easiest to map it using GPS coordinates.

Luckily, Google has a system of codes that converts the coordinates into pin-drop locations that Google Maps can interpret and navigate.

Each adventure in this guide includes GPS coordinates along with a physical address whenever it is available.

It is important that you are prepared for poor cell signals. It is recommended that you route your location and ensure that the directions are accessible offline. Depending on your device and the distance of some locations, you may need to travel with a backup battery source.

About Louisiana

Known as the Pelican State, Louisiana was the eighteenth state to join the Union. Louisiana's history is a foundational part of U.S. history. With so much diversity in cuisine, entertainment, and culture, Louisiana is one of the most heavily visited states in America. It offers so much for such a variety of people that there is something for everyone in the Gulf Coast state.

The Louisiana Territory was once occupied by two prominent Native American tribes: the Plaquemine and the Caddoan. These two tribes established a vibrant culture of commerce and trade dating as far back as the 1200s to 1600s. They still occupied the land when the first Europeans came to the lower Mississippi region.

In 1528, explorers from Spain were the first Europeans to set foot in Louisiana. Led by Panfilo de Narvaez, the Spanish expedition sailed down the Mississippi River to the Gulf of Mexico.

About 150 years later, French and French-Canadian explorers came down the Mississippi, and, when they arrived at the river delta region, they were taken by it and began to establish the land as their own. The French idea was to claim a huge expanse of land that would be French-owned and would connect Canada and the Gulf of Mexico. In 1682, French explorer Robert Cavelier de La Salle named the area Louisiana after King Louis XIV of France. Soon a lucrative trade business began from Canada to the south as the French occupied most of what is now the United States between the Rocky Mountains and the Alleghenies. Before long, the French brought the slave trade to Louisiana and that brought with it a migration from Haiti. This is where Louisiana gets its Creole influence and cuisine.

In 1803, to pay back debts owed to the United States, France sold the Louisiana Territory for $3.4 million in the famous Louisiana Purchase. From then on, America expanded west and broadened its borders.

On April 30, 1812, the Territory of Orleans officially became the state of Louisiana. Louisiana would be a central location during the American Civil War and the Civil Rights movement of the twentieth century.

Landscape and Climate

Louisiana is also known as the Bayou State because of its various bayous, marshlands, and wetlands along the gulf. As you travel further north into Louisiana, you will find a more mountainous landscape. The entire western part of the state sits on the Mississippi River and the southern part on the Gulf of Mexico, which gives Louisiana beaches and barrier islands. The most unique feature of the Louisiana landscape is that from the gulf toward the middle of the state, the land slopes down in some areas below sea level. This has been hazardous in Louisiana's history, as seen in the summer of 2005 when Hurricane Katrina made landfall near New Orleans, submerging the city and the southern part of the state under water. Louisiana's geographic location and subtropical climate make it highly susceptible to hurricanes and tropical storms. The average temperature in the summer is about 90° F, with temperatures around 65° F in the winter months.

Palmetto Island State Park

Palmetto Island State Park is located on the Vermilion River. The park is known for its palmettos and nature-rich, interior lagoons. The 943-acres includes a 50-ft observation tower for wildlife viewing. A boat launch makes it easy to take to the water for fishing and exploring. You can rent a kayak or a canoe and follow trails through the lagoons, where you can get close to the native plant life and wildlife of this part of the state.

There are ninety-six campsites and an RV park with six cabins in the park that fit up to eight people comfortably. Each cabin is complete with a kitchen, bathroom, fireplaces, and screened-in porches. There is a visitor center that includes a bathhouse, multipurpose room, a park, and a scavenger hunt of the grounds.

Best Time to Visit: Palmetto Island State Park is open and accessible year-round.

Pass/Permit/Fees: It costs $3 to enter the park. Children under age 3 are free, as well as adults 62 and over.

Closest City or Town: Abbeville

Address: 19501 Pleasant Rd., Abbeville, LA 70510

GPS Coordinates: 29.5871° N, 97.5822° W

Did You Know? The idea of the park was conceived in 1981 but wasn't built until 2002. After many delays, it opened in 2010.

Chicot State Park

Chicot State Park is located in the south-central part of Louisiana. It features 6,400 acres of parks, trees, and wilderness. Within the park, there is a 2,000-acre man-made lake that is filled with fish and has become a popular fishing hole with residents.

Lake Chicot is surrounded by a hiking/backpack trail that has campsites throughout. The trail is also used by mountain bikers and cyclists. The lake has three landings. The south landing is where the playgrounds and docks are, as well as campsites, a waterpark, and picnic areas.

The north landing has a boat launch and some camping. The east landing is very underdeveloped but offers a boat landing, BBQ area, and meeting area.

Best Time to Visit: Chicot Park is accessible year-round between the hours of 6 a.m. and 10 p.m.

Pass/Permit/Fees: It costs $3 to enter Chicot State Park. Children under age 3 and adults over 62 are free.

Closest City or Town: Alexandria

Address: 3469 Chicot Park Rd., Ville Platte, LA 70586

GPS Coordinates: 30° 48.0168 N 92° 16.7832 W

Did You Know? While in the park, you may see several mammal species, including bobcats, coyotes, whitetail deer, and raccoons.

Kisatchie National Forest

Kisatchie National Forest consists of 600,000 acres of land in central Louisiana. The forest is located in seven different parishes in Louisiana, and it is the largest protected land in the state. It offers visitors every kind of outdoor activity including, fishing, hiking, camping, birding, swimming, boating, viewing, and hunting. It is free to enjoy this national land, but always check to make sure you don't need a permit to do something specific as that may cost some money.

There are over 100 miles of hiking trails in the forest that give stunning views of the Louisiana landscape. There are also several camping sites throughout the park where you can camp either in a tent under the stars or in an RV. As you go through the park, you will see magnolias, pines, and evergreens, and you may spot a turkey, armadillo, raccoon, or deer.

Best Time to Visit: Kisatchie is open and accessible year-round.

Pass/Permit/Fees: It is free to enter Kisatchie National Forest.

Closest City or Town: Alexandria

Address: 2500 Shreveport Hwy., Pineville, LA 71360

GPS Coordinates: 31.2020° N, 92.2445° W

Did You Know? Kisatchie National Forest is the only national forest in Louisiana.

Natchitoches

Natchitoches is the oldest city in Louisiana. After the Louisiana Purchase, it was the first settlement founded in 1714. What makes Natchitoches so unique is that it never lost its flair, architecture, or influence from Europe.

Cane River runs through Natchitoches, offering a variety of water sports, including paddling. There is also a shooting range in Natchitoches as well as a golf course, skating, tennis, and a pool. There are riverboat cruises you can take down the Cane River.

The Briarwood Nature Preserve is located in Natchitoches, which offers a wildlife sanctuary for all to enjoy. The Natchitoches area is home to Caroline Dorman, the first woman hired by the United States Forest Service.

Best Time to Visit: Natchitoches is accessible and fun all year long.

Pass/Permit/Fees: It is free to visit Natchitoches, but any excursions may have a fee.

Closest City or Town: Alexandria

Address: Natchitoches, LA 71497

GPS Coordinates: 31.7607° N, 93.0863° W

Did You Know? Natchitoches is home to the Louisiana Sports Hall of Fame.

South Toledo Bend State Park

South Toledo Bend State Park is home to popular bass fishing tournaments. Avid fishing enthusiasts can come to the reservoir and catch bass, bream, and white perch. There are also plenty of land activities available, including cycling and hiking. There is a 3,000-foot trail that loops around the reservoir and the area near the visitor center. A breezeway passes through the park and ends at an observation deck where you get stunning views of the nearby islands and the reservoir. Around the visitor center, you will find several picnic areas to have lunch and take in the scenery.

There are overnight camping options at South Toledo Bend State Park. The park includes campsites and an RV park. There are also nineteen two-bedroom cabins. Each cabin sleeps eight and includes a full kitchen, bathroom, and back deck.

Best Time to Visit: South Toledo Bend State Park is open and accessible year-round.

Pass/Permit/Fees: It costs $3 to enter the park. Children under age 3 are free, as well as adults 62 and over.

Closest City or Town: Anacoco

Address: 120 Bald Eagle, Anacoco, LA 71403

GPS Coordinates: 31.1229° N, 93.3412° W

Did You Know? South Toledo Bend State Park is a popular nesting ground for bald eagles.

Atchafalaya Basin

Atchafalaya is a major swamp in south-central Louisiana and the largest swamp in the United States. The swamp is formed where the Atchafalaya River meets the Gulf of Mexico. The basin contains bayous, marshes, and cypress swamps. The basin's open water has been decreasing over time. In the mid to late twentieth century, oil and gas lines were placed throughout the swamp, which changed its balance, though it seems to be stabilizing as its delta system continues to grow.

The Bayou Chene was a town that thrived on the success of fishing, hunting, trapping, and logging. The town is now a ghost town that is covered in about 12 feet of silt. The basin is best used for hunting, fishing, trapping, and camping.

Best Time to Visit: The Atchafalaya Basin is accessible year-round but can flood in the spring and winter.

Pass/Permit/Fees: It is free to enter the basin, but any tours or permits may cost a fee.

Closest City or Town: Baton Rouge

Address: 1908 Atchafalaya River Hwy., Breaux Bridge, LA 70517

GPS Coordinates: 30.3696° N, 91.6526° W

Did You Know? The Atchafalaya Basin has 260,000 acres of cypress-tupelo swamps. That is the largest contiguous area of coastal cypress in America.

Atchafalaya National Heritage Area

Atchafalaya National Heritage Area is a place of deep history for the people of Louisiana. It is an area that not only preserves wildlife but also holds events for people. It is located in the Atchafalaya Basin, which is the largest freshwater swamp area in the United States. In the park, you will see black bears, muskrats, beavers, otters, and raccoons.

There are sixty-five species of amphibians and 250 species of birds. The area hosts many culturally-rich concerts, including one that is dedicated to the music of the Acadian population. There are also farmers' markets where you can buy from local merchants. The area is used for tours, boating, hunting, fishing, and paddling.

Best Time to Visit: The area is accessible year-round, but there may be flooding in the spring and winter.

Pass/Permit/Fees: It is free to enjoy the trails and natural wonders of Atchafalaya. There may be a cost to do tours or other excursions.

Closest City or Town: Baton Rouge

Address: 2022 Atchafalaya River Hwy., Breaux Bridge, LA 70517

GPS Coordinates: 30.3415° N, 91.7229° W

Did You Know? Atchafalaya Heritage Area is home to the largest nesting ground for the bald eagle in the southeastern United States.

Baton Rouge

Baton Rouge is the capital city of Louisiana. The name comes from the French for "red stick." The city sits on the Mississippi River and was built on the Istrouma Bluff, which is a natural bluff that protects Baton Rouge from seasonal flooding. To further fortify the city, levees were built to the south to protect the expanding downtown area from rising waters.

It is believed that human life has been in the Baton Rouge area since 12000 – 6500 BC based on mounds built in the area that are indicative of hunter-gatherer societies. Baton Rouge was named by Pierre La Moyne, who also named Lake Pontchartrain and Lake Maurepas during the French colonial period.

Best Time to Visit: Baton Rouge is accessible and enjoyable all year long.

Pass/Permit/Fees: It is free to visit Baton Rouge, but some local attractions may have a fee.

Closest City or Town: The next biggest city to Baton Rouge is New Orleans.

Address: Baton Rouge, LA 70808

GPS Coordinates: 30.4515° N, 91.1871° W

Did You Know? Baton Rouge is the ninety-ninth most populous city in the United States.

False River

False River gets its name because it was once a river but is now an oxbow lake. Until 1722, False River was a part of the Mississippi. When the mighty river changed course, it left a 10.5-mile-long lake now known as False River. Known for its crystal-clear waters, this lake is famous for its bass fishing and is referred to as a "trophy lake." Most of the fishing is catch-and-release, encouraging the fish to continue growing to impressive sizes. In addition to fishing, water skiing, sailing, and boating are also popular activities.

On the False River shore, the historic LeJeune House still stands. The 200-year-old home sits on what was once a 500-acre plantation. The Library of Congress has archived measured drawings of the house as part of the Historic American Building Survey. The LeJeune House is recognized as the oldest home in the area.

Best Time to Visit: False Lake is accessible year-round.

Pass/Permit/Fees: It is free to enjoy False River.

Closest City or Town: Baton Rouge

Address: 2050 False River Dr., New Roads, LA 70760

GPS Coordinates: 30.3819° N, 91.2904° W

Did You Know? False River typically holds the state record for the catch of the largest bass and the most bass per acre

Horace Wilkinson Bridge

Named after three different Horace Wilkinsons, the Horace Wilkinson Bridge is a tribute to three men who served in the Louisiana State Legislature for a total of 54 years. The three men are Horace Wilkinson, his son, and his grandson, who all share the same name. The bridge was built and named in 1968. It is a cantilever bridge that is about 14,150 feet long. It spans six lanes of traffic and is one of two heavily trafficked bridges going into and out of Baton Rouge. The bridge begins in Port Allen by an exit for Louisiana State Highway 1 and continues over the Mississippi River into the state capital of Baton Rouge near the campus for Louisiana State University. It has the nickname "the new bridge" because it is the newest of two bridges that cross the river in Baton Rouge. The other older bridge is the Huey P. Long Bridge, named after the 40th governor of Louisiana.

Best Time to Visit: The Horace Wilkinson Bridge is open all year long.

Pass/Permit/Fees: It is free to drive over the Horace Wilkinson Bridge.

Closest City or Town: Baton Rouge

Address: I-10, Baton Rouge, LA 70802

GPS Coordinates: 30.4395° N, 91.1957° W

Did You Know? The Horace Wilkinson Bridge is the highest bridge that crosses the Mississippi River at 175 feet above the water.

LSU Rural Life Museum

The Rural Life Museum, run by Louisiana State University, depicts rural life throughout the varied history of Louisiana. A lot of the buildings on the site are from the eighteenth and nineteenth centuries, and they give a very good idea of what life was like during that time.

The plantation section of the grounds shows what life could have been like during the time of working plantations. There are several buildings you can see, such as the sick house, the schoolhouse, the blacksmith, grist mill, and sugar house.

There is also a section representing early American settlers in the northern part of Louisiana, and the museum shows artifacts and details of the ways of life for Cajun and Acadian culture.

Best Time to Visit: The museum is open and accessible all year long. It is closed on major holidays.

Pass/Permit/Fees: Tickets are $10 for adults ages 12 - 61 and $8 for children ages 6 - 11.

Closest City or Town: Baton Rouge

Address: 4560 Essen Ln., Baton Rouge, LA 70808

GPS Coordinates: 34.4057° N, 91.1035° W

Did You Know? There is a botanical garden on the site. The Windrush Gardens costs an additional $3 to enter.

Magnolia Mound Plantation

Magnolia Mound Plantation was a source of sugarcane, tobacco, cotton, and indigo. The land was originally owned by a Scottish family who ran the plantation with five slaves. Later in history, the land would be purchased by an Irishman who would increase the number of slaves to fifty. The owner eventually died in a boating accident while he was sailing from New Orleans to Mobile. His widow remarried and had five more children. Because the family grew so big, the house and the grounds were expanded. Eventually, in the twentieth century, the city of Baton Rouge took over the land, and it is now a historic site. Today, you can take tours of Magnolia Mound and learn about enslaved communities, life on the plantation, and how early Americans lived. There are several structures on the plantation that you can visit, including the slave quarters.

Best Time to Visit: Magnolia Mound is open and accessible all year long.

Pass/Permit/Fees: Tickets cost $10 for adults and $4 for children ages 3 - 17.

Closest City or Town: Baton Rouge

Address: 2161 Nicholson Dr., Baton Rouge, LA 70802

GPS Coordinates: 30.4262° N, 91.1872° W

Did You Know? The main plantation house, which started as just a cottage, was one of the first buildings constructed in modern-day Baton Rouge.

Mississippi River

Running from Lake Itasca in Minnesota down to the Gulf of Mexico, the Mississippi River is considered to be the dividing line between the American east and west. The river runs 2,318 miles and is the second-longest river (next to the Missouri River) and drainage system in North America. During the Civil War, the Union took control of the river, and this was a turning point for the North. The river was a major waterway for transporting goods to the south via steamboats and river boats. The Mississippi River has also been the inspiration for classic American songs like "Old Man River." The Mississippi River also played a major role in westward expansion. There are many tributaries that run off the river, followed by explorers seeking to discover new land.

Best Time to Visit: Anytime

Pass/Permit/Fees: The Mississippi River is free to enjoy.

Closest City or Town: Baton Rouge

Address: In Baton Rouge, the Mississippi River is along River Road, right next to the Louisiana State Capitol Building.

GPS Coordinates: 35° 30' 52.9416" N and 89° 54' 45.0216" W

Did You Know? The river flows through or borders ten states, which are Minnesota, Iowa, Wisconsin, Illinois, Kentucky, Missouri, Tennessee, Arkansas, Mississippi, and Louisiana.

Old Arsenal Museum

The Old Arsenal Museum depicts the history of the arsenal and the role it has played in Louisiana. It is considered the most historic part of Baton Rouge. Originally known as the Powder Magazine, it was a military outpost during the Battle of Baton Rouge and would go on to be a popular spot for military action due to its location on the Mississippi River.

Before the onset of the Civil War, the arsenal was the home base of the Louisiana militia that would soon break off from the Union to become a free territory before joining the Confederate States of America.

Union troops occupied the spot during the Civil War at the Battle of Baton Rouge. Now, it stands on the same ground as the New State Capitol.

Best Time to Visit: The museum is open on Thursdays. It can be accessed by appointment only the rest of the week.

Pass/Permit/Fees: It is free to enjoy the museum.

Closest City or Town: Baton Rouge

Address: 900 Capitol Lake Dr., Baton Rouge, LA 70802

GPS Coordinates: 30.4585° N, 91.1847° W

Did You Know? Graffiti from the time of the Civil War is still on the walls of the arsenal.

Old Louisiana Governor's Mansion

The Old Louisiana Governor's Mansion was built in the 1920s by Louisiana governor Huey P. Long. Long was the first governor to live in the mansion, which was then home to all subsequent Louisiana governors until 1963 when a new residence was built. The mansion is located in Baton Rouge, the state's capital. Governor Long had the old Knox Mansion completely disassembled by a team of convicted criminals under his orders as governor.

The next day, plans were approved for the new mansion that took about two years to build. This incident was one of many that were part of Governor Long's impeachment proceedings later in the 1930s. The mansion is a historic landmark, and you can take tours to see its chandeliers, velvet curtains, and luxurious furniture and construction.

Best Time to Visit: The mansion is open Tuesday through Friday.

Pass/Permit/Fees: Ticket prices are $10 for adults, $9 for seniors, and $8 for children 5 and older.

Closest City or Town: Baton Rouge

Address: 502 North Blvd., Baton Rouge, LA 70802

GPS Coordinates: 30.4466° N, 91.1849° W

Did You Know? Governor Huey P. Long was so convinced he was going to be president one day that he had the mansion designed after the White House so he could get used to being there.

Old State Capitol

Old State Capitol is now a museum that tells of the colorful history of Louisiana. The mission of the museum is to inspire citizenship and pride in being part of Louisiana. There are several tours and exhibits that depict Louisiana's most poignant historical moments. Designed to look like a castle, the capitol was built when Baton Rouge was selected as the capital city. When Union troops took over Baton Rouge during the Civil War, a fire broke out that gutted the building. When the war ended, the building was repaired and used once again until the 1930s, when a new state capitol was built. Many organizations have inhabited the building over the years, and in 1976 it became a historic landmark and, eventually, a museum.

Best Time to Visit: The museum is open Monday through Saturday.

Pass/Permit/Fees: It is free to enter the museum and take tours. There is a short movie that you can watch about the museum's history that costs $3.

Closest City or Town: Baton Rouge

Address: 100 North Blvd., Baton Rouge, LA 70801

GPS Coordinates: 39.4823° N, 89.3832° W

Did You Know? It's been said that the day Louisiana chose to secede from the U.S., the biggest cheer ever heard came from the capitol. Louisiana was an independent state for two months before joining the Confederacy.

Rosedown Plantation and Gardens

Rosedown Plantation was owned and operated by Daniel and Martha Turnbull. Daniel became the wealthiest man in the United States for his time. He acquired the land that is now Rosedown Plantation through several land purchases from the 1820s through the 1840s. The main house of the plantation was built between 1834 and 1835. The house would be furnished with the finest pieces that could be found from North America and Europe. While the Turnbulls honeymooned in Europe, Martha was inspired by the royal gardens, and over many years, she constructed a replica on the property. Today, you can tour the grounds and the house. At one point, there were 450 slaves on the plantation harvesting cotton, and today you can tour the thirteen buildings that remain, including the house. In 2005, Rosedown became a National Landmark.

Best Time to Visit: Rosedown Plantation is accessible all year long.

Pass/Permit/Fees: It costs $12 for adults and $6 for children ages 4 – 17 to tour the house and grounds. To just tour the grounds, the fee for adults is $7, while the fee for children ages 4 – 17 is $5.

Closest City or Town: Baton Rouge

Address: 12501 LA-10, St. Francisville, LA 70775

GPS Coordinates: 30.7960° N, 91.3709° W

Did You Know? The plantation was named Rosedown after a play the Turnbulls saw on their honeymoon.

The Myrtles Plantation

The Myrtles Plantation is located in St. Francisville. It was built in 1796 by General David Bradford. He lived there after he was pardoned for his role in the Whiskey Rebellion by President John Adams. It is built in the Creole cottage-style that was very popular in Louisiana in the 1790s. The house was expanded upon in the 1850s, doubling the size of the structure. The doorways have panels of hand-painted glass designed after the French cross, which was produced to ward off evil. There are twenty-two rooms in the house with five bedrooms, and each bedroom has its own bathroom. The windows and floors are all original. There is a small pond with an island in the middle that has a gazebo you can access by a small bridge. Today, the house is used for tours and as a hotel for overnight guests.

Best Time to Visit: The Myrtles is open and accessible all year long.

Pass/Permit/Fees: Tour prices vary but generally cost $15 per person.

Closest City or Town: Baton Rouge

Address: 7747 US-61, St. Francisville, LA 70775

GPS Coordinates: 30.4811° N, 91.2315° W

Did You Know? Myrtles Plantation is one of the most haunted houses in America. It is built on a Native American burial site, and the ghost of a young Native American woman has been seen in the house.

USS Kidd and Veterans Memorial

The *USS Kidd* is a Fletcher-class destroyer for the United States Navy that was built in Kearny, New Jersey but is now docked on the Mississippi River in Baton Rouge. The *USS Kidd* served the United States in the Pacific Ocean during World War II and the Korean War. In 1945, it suffered severe damage off the coast of Okinawa in Japan.

By the 1970s, it was deemed unfit for service and was retired as a veterans' memorial in Baton Rouge. It is the only former Navy ship to be completely renovated to its original condition from the 1940s. Today, the *USS Kidd* is a veterans' memorial where you can learn about the courage of the brave men and women that served the United States. You can sleep on the ship overnight, have birthday parties there, and book other events.

Best Time to Visit: Open and available year-round.

Pass/Permit/Fees: Entry fees for adults are $12.53, for children are $8.36, and for veterans and seniors are $10.45.

Closest City or Town: Baton Rouge

Address: 305 S. River Rd., Baton Rouge, LA 70802

GPS Coordinates: 30.2640° N, 91.1129° W.

Did You Know? The *USS Kidd* was named after Rear Admiral Isaac Campbell Kidd, Sr., who was killed during the Pearl Harbor Attack on December 7, 1941. He was the first American casualty of WWII.

St. Bernard State Park

St. Bernard State Park is very close to the city of New Orleans, so the location is perfect for campers who want to be close to a busy, cultural area. Located on the Mississippi River, the park is known for its man-made lagoons. Although most of the animal life is small and docile—rabbits, raccoons, opossums, squirrels, and turtles—there are alligators, so keep an eye out as you boat and explore.

The park includes 51 camp sites which include water, electrical hook-ups, picnic tables, and barbeque grills. There is a bathhouse with hot showers and laundry facilities available for guests to make this the perfect mix between nature and comfort. Pets are allowed to camp, but they are prohibited from joining their owners in the buildings.

Best Time to Visit: St. Bernard State Park is open and accessible year-round.

Pass/Permit/Fees: It costs $2 per person ages 16 and older and $1 per person ages 15 and under.

Closest City or Town: Braithwaite

Address: 501 St. Bernard Pkwy., Braithwaite, LA 70040

GPS Coordinates: 29.8613° N, 89.9008° W

Did You Know? The land that is now St. Bernard State Park was owned by a local family business. The land to create the park was donated for public use in 1971.

Bayou Segnette State Park

Bayou Segnette State Park is located across the Mississippi River from New Orleans. Located on the bayou, this state park is composed of swamp and marshland. While in the park, you can boat, camp, canoe, hike, and picnic. There are also playgrounds for kids and a waterpark.

The fishing in the area is unique in variety because the park is located near freshwater and saltwater. You can catch bass, catfish, perch, redfish, bream, and trout. You will also be able to see animals from both marshlands and wetlands.

For hikers, there is a 2.8-mile trail accessible, and for those who want to make a day and night out of their visit, cabins are available on the water to rent. The 98 campsites within the park include water and electrical hook-ups. Before exploring this area, it is important to keep in mind that most cell phones do not receive service in the park.

Best Time to Visit: The park is accessible year-round between the hours of 7 a.m. and 10 p.m.

Pass/Permit/Fees: It costs $3 to enter the park. Seniors over 62 years old and children under 3 are free.

Closest City or Town: Bridge City

Address: 7777 Westbank Expy., Westwego, LA 70094

GPS Coordinates: 29.8923° N, 90.1634° W

Did You Know? Bayou Segnette State Park has a wave pool. You can spend the day riding waves in the waterpark.

Lake Bistineau State Park

Located on the western shore of Lake Bistineau, Lake Bistineau State Park is known for its magical cypress and tupelo trees surrounding the lake. The park offers boating, biking, hiking, camping, playgrounds and is a popular site for fishing. There are yellow bass, bluegill, red-ear sunfish, largemouth bass, and catfish in the water.

The lake has a surface area of 26.9 square miles and is between 7 and 25 feet deep. There are several trails to enjoy on foot or by bicycle, and the lake also has a canoe trail for kayakers and canoers to enjoy. The park offers cabin rentals which include bedrooms, bathrooms, fully equipped kitchens, central air conditioning, and heat.

Best Time to Visit: Lake Bistineau State Park is open year-round between the hours of 8 a.m. and 10 p.m.

Pass/Permit/Fees: It costs $3 to enter the park. Children under age 3 and seniors over 62 are free.

Closest City or Town: Doyline

Address: 103 State Park Rd., Doyline, LA 71023

GPS Coordinates: 32.2623° N, 93.2229° W

Did You Know? Lake Bistineau is over 200 years old. The lake was originally formed around 1800 when there was a massive flood formed the river. The flood wasn't created by nature. It was formed by man when a huge log jam caused the Red River to overflow its banks.

Poverty Point

Poverty Point is designated as a U.S. National Monument. The area resembles an amphitheater structure and is located about 15.5 miles from the banks of the Mississippi River. The area consists of about 402 acres but was constructed over the course of several years and generations. Built around the same time as Stonehenge, Native Americans built the 72-foot-tall mound and landscaped the terrain by hand. It remained the largest earthen monument in the area for over two thousand years!

Today, it is still a mystery as to why the natural owners abandoned the site around 1100 B.C. In the 1800s, 2,900 years later, Euroamericans immigrated to the region. Poverty Point was recognized as a National Historic Landmark in 1962, and in 2014 UNESCO honored it as a World Heritage Site.

Best Time to Visit: Poverty Point is accessible year-round except on major holidays.

Pass/Permit/Fees: It costs $4 to enter the monument. Children under age 12 and adults 62 and over are free.

Closest City or Town: Epps

Address: 6859 LA-577, Pioneer, LA 71266

GPS Coordinates: 32.3812° N, 91.2441° W

Did You Know? No one quite knows what the area was used for, but many archeologists believe it was used as either a trading center or a place for religious ceremonies.

Cajun French Music Hall of Fame and Museum

The Cajun French Music Hall of Fame and Museum tells stories about the roots of Cajun music in the United States. The museum delves back into the history of the genre and the men and women who were the pioneers of the music many in the South and the world have come to know and love.

The museum is located in Eunice in St. Landry Parish. Eunice is in the heart of Cajun country and hosts many Cajun festivals. The exhibits in the museum reflect some of the greatest Cajun musicians, including Joe Falcon, Denis McGee, and Iry Lejeune.

There is a special exhibit about the first female artist to record Cajun music, Cleoma Falcon. There is another in-depth exhibit about the current female artists in the genre.

Best Time to Visit: The museum is open and accessible all year long. It is closed on Sundays and Mondays.

Pass/Permit/Fees: It is free to visit the museum

Closest City or Town: Eunice

Address: 240 S C C Duson St., Eunice, LA 70535

GPS Coordinates: 30.4912° N, 92.4251° W

Did You Know? There are 141 musicians and disc jockeys inducted into the Hall of Fame. Every year six new members out of ten are inducted.

Lake D'Arbonne State Park

Lake D'Arbonne is a top fishing area in Louisiana. It's a man-made reservoir with five fishing piers to enjoy. Locals and tourists alike often catch bass, crappie, catfish, and bream in the pristine waters. The lake is 15,250 acres of water surrounded by pines and trails that are popular with cyclists and hikers. Surrounding the lake, the massive pines support tree stands for photographers and birdwatchers to immerse themselves in the Louisiana wilderness.

There are picnic areas around the lake for barbecuing as well as lighted tennis courts to allow playing at night. With 65 campsites, 18 vacation cabins, two lodges, and a group camp that allows for 52 guests, this is an ideal location for family getaways as well as collective excursions.

Best Time to Visit: Lake D'Arbonne State Park is accessible year-round.

Pass/Permit/Fees: It costs $3 to enter the park. Children under age 3 and adults 62 and over are free. There is a cost for camping and activities.

Closest City or Town: Farmerville

Address: 3628 Evergreen Rd., Farmerville, LA 7124

GPS Coordinates: 32.7564° N, 92.4323° W

Did You Know? The idea for the lake was conceived in 1957. A dam was built to stop the flow of water in 1961, and by 1963, the lake was formed.

Bogue Chitto State Park

At Bogue Chitto State Park, visitors can enjoy hiking and camping as well as 14 miles of equestrian riding. The park features 1,786 acres of swamps, forests, and streams. Cypress-tupelo swamps and hardwood forests surround eleven fully stocked lakes, water playgrounds, and picnic pavilions. In addition to five cabins, there are RV sites, a conference center, a group camp, a canoe launch, and an amphitheater.

One of the most unique and alluring attributes of this state park is Fricke's Cave. The cave is less of a cave and more of a gorge known for its sandstone spires topped with pebbles. Visitors can see the spires from the boardwalks webbing the area.

Best Time to Visit: Bogue Chitto State Park is open all year round between the hours of 8 AM and 10 PM.

Pass/Permit/Fees: It costs $3 to enter Bogue Chitto State Park. It is free for children under 3 and seniors over 62.

Closest City or Town: Franklinton

Address: 17049 State Park Blvd., Franklinton, LA 70438

GPS Coordinates: 30.7675° N, 90.1573070°W

Did You Know? Fourteen miles of mountain bike and equestrian trails, designated for all skill levels, wind through the park. In addition to this, there are opportunities to rent cabins overlooking a ninety-foot bluff within the park.

Grand Isle

Grand Isle is Louisiana's only inhabited barrier island. Located on the Gulf of Mexico, about two hours from New Orleans, the island is known for its delicious array of seafood cuisine, fishing, and bird migrations. In addition to its nightlife, public parks, and beaches, many visitors come for the onshore fishing as there are over 280 species found off the coast. Grand Isle is home to seven miles of public beaches, which are accessed from "crossovers" over these lanes: Olive, Jean Lafitte, Boudreaux, Cranberry, Apple, Krantz, Capital, Chighizola, Coulon Rigaud, Post, Landry, Oak, Cypress, Birch, and Humble Road. Each crossover has its own parking lot to make access easier. For wildlife enthusiasts, Elmer's Island Wildlife Refuge is a 230-acre stretch of barrier beachfront located across Caminada Pass. This refuge is home to beaches, a tidal zone, mangrove and saltwater marshes, and dunes. It is recommended to check online before planning a visit as they will close the refuge during rehabilitation after hurricanes.

Best Time to Visit: Grand Isle can be enjoyed year-round.

Pass/Permit/Fees: It is free to visit Grand Isle, but all activities cost money.

Closest City or Town: Galliano

Address: 108 Admiral Craik Dr., Grand Isle, LA 70358

GPS Coordinates: 29.2366° N, 89.9873° W

Did You Know? Grand Isle is known as the "Sportsman's Paradise" because of the ample wildlife in the area.

Houmas House Plantation and Gardens

Houmas House Plantation and Gardens is located on the Mississippi River in Darrow. It has had several owners over the course of the past 400 years. The location is on naturally high ground and has been used to harvest sugar cane, tobacco, cotton, indigo, and corn.

The first French house was built in the 1700s, and for the next 200 years, it would be expanded, and the house would grow into a mansion. Today, Houmas House is a place where you can tour the grounds, see the gardens, and have private events, including weddings.

There is also an inn on the property where you can stay and enjoy the surroundings. There are top-notch restaurants on the grounds for eating and drinking as well.

Best Time to Visit: Houmas House is open and accessible all year long.

Pass/Permit/Fees: There are several tours you can take through the plantation. The price depends on which tour you choose.

Closest City or Town: Gonzales

Address: 40136 LA-942, Darrow, LA 70725

GPS Coordinates: 30.1407° N, 90.9351° W

Did You Know? Houmas House gets its name from the Native American tribe that used to live on the land.

Bayou Terrebonne Waterlife Museum

The Bayou Terrebonne Waterlife Museum is a museum completely dedicated to the waters of the bayou and reveals the way transportation and commerce have affected the lives of everyone who lives in the region. The museum has artifacts and displays that depict the ties between the people and the industries that were created because of the bayou, from seafood to water transportation to hunting and gathering and mining. While visiting the museum, you will see a 46-foot-long wall that shows a detailed timeline of the region's eco-line from the beginning of time to the present. It is depicted through a large mural of life-sized renditions of the plants and animals of the region. There is also an exhibition where you can learn about the fur and alligator industries of the bayou. Other displays speak to commerce and industry created from the water system.

Best Time to Visit: The Bayou Terrebonne Museum is open Tuesday through Saturday.

Pass/Permit/Fees: Adults pay $3 and children ages 2 - 11 pay $2.

Closest City or Town: Houma

Address: 7910 W. Park Ave., Houma, LA 70364

GPS Coordinates: 29.3554° N, 90.4313°W

Did You Know? There is a life-sized, interactive alligator in the museum that you can play with as you learn about alligators. Alligator hunting is part of the rich history of the bayou.

Kenny Hill's Sculpture Garden

Kenny Hill believed that he was divinely told to create this garden so that other people could learn about God through his own sins. The garden is filled with concrete statues of angels that represent religious lessons. Some of the depictions show angels being kicked out of Heaven and winged angels with halos that are lit by fluorescent lights. Some of the sculptures depict the Rapture.

Kenny Hill began to build a 45-foot lighthouse covered with religious imagery. He put himself into some of the statues as a nod toward his inner struggles. There are several depictions of himself trying to reach God but failing. In 2000, Kenny Hill stopped working on the garden, and it has since been taken over by a local university that takes care of the art.

Best Time to Visit: Kenny Hill sculpture garden is open all year long.

Pass/Permit/Fees: It is free to enter the garden, but guided tours may cost a fee.

Closest City or Town: Houma

Address: 5337 Bayouside Dr., Chauvin, LA 70344

GPS Coordinates: 29.4439° N, 90.5930° W

Did You Know? Kenny Hill had a crisis of faith and decided to stop working on the garden while he was in the middle of making two angel statues. He kicked the head off a statue of Jesus and left town, never to be seen again.

Southdown Museum

Southdown Museum was primarily used as a sugar plantation in the 19th century. The main house is filled with several artifacts and historical items from the time the plantation was in full use. There are self-guided tours that you can take of the workman's house and guided tours of the plantation house and quarters of the enslaved workers. The plantation is also used for events. The plantation was founded in 1828 by Stephen Minor, who used to work for the Spanish Governor of Louisiana. Minor began growing indigo, but by 1831 he began to harvest sugar cane and then eventually built a sugar mill on the property. After the Great Depression, the family lost the house, and it became a historic landmark. In 1982, the grounds became a museum.

Best Time to Visit: Southdown Plantation is open and accessible all year long.

Pass/Permit/Fees: Tours must be scheduled, and ticket prices are $17 for adults, $10 for children ages 14 - 17, and $8 for children ages 5 - 13.

Closest City or Town: Houma

Address: 1208 Museum Dr., Houma, LA 70360

GPS Coordinates: 29.5882° N, 90.7401° W

Did You Know? When the sugar mill closed, the parts were disassembled and shipped to Guatemala, where they were reassembled and used to make sugar in Central America.

Breaux Bridge

Located in south-central Louisiana, Breaux Bridge is famous for its annual crawfish festival. In 1771, Firmin Breaux purchased the land that is now Breaux Bridge. Its name comes from a footbridge spanning over Bayou Teche that Breaux built in 1799. The suspension bridge was originally installed for personal use to make it easier for friends and family to visit. His son improved the bridge in 1817, allowing for wagons to transport over the Bayou. It was not until 1829, after Firmin's death, that his widow officially founded the town of Breaux Bridge. When restaurants opened in the city, they were the first in Louisiana to list crawfish on the menu. This eventually grew to the point where crawfish farming became a central part of the Breaux Bridge economy. In 1959, the city hosted the first annual crawfish festival as part of its centennial celebration. Today, it is a bustling town of shops and dining establishments. If you decide to visit, it is recommended to sample the famous crawfish etouffee.

Best Time to Visit: Breaux Bridge is accessible year-round.

Pass/Permit/Fees: It is free to enter the town.

Closest City or Town: Lafayette

Address: Breaux Bridge, LA 70517

GPS Coordinates: 30.2735° N, 91.8993° W

Did You Know? Breaux Bridge was recognized by the legislature as the "Crawfish Capital of the World."

Cypress Island Preserve

Cypress Island Preserve is located on Lake Martin. The lake offers swimming, boating, waterskiing, jet skiing, and fishing. Lake Martin has one of the biggest cypress-tupelo swamps in the southern United States of about 565 acres. The Cypress Island Preserve helps keep that swamp intact and safe.

The entire area of the preserve is about 10,000 acres of bottomland hardwood forest and swamp. There is a bird conservatory on site that houses nesting and rookery for several species of birds.

The roseate spoonbill, herons, egrets, and ibis can be found throughout the year on the lake. You can see these birds from the hiking trail that goes through the preserve.

Best Time to Visit: The Cypress Island Preserve is accessible and open year-round.

Pass/Permit/Fees: It is free to enter Cypress Island Preserve.

Closest City or Town: Lafayette

Address: 1264 Prairie Hwy., St. Martinville, LA 70582

GPS Coordinates: 26.0485° N, 81.0754° W

Did You Know? Lake Martin was originally called Lake la Pointe. It would dry out in the summer, so a levee was built to hold the water year-round.

Lake Martin

Lake Martin is the home of Cypress Island Nature Preserve, a swampy forest, which is home to several species of birds. As the state's largest nesting colony, visitors can hope to spot the Anhinga, Great Egret, Great Blue Heron, Snowy Egret, Little Blue Heron, Tri-colored Heron, Cattle Egret, Black-crowned Night Heron, White Ibis, and Roseate Spoonbill. It is not only nesting ground for water birds but alligators as well. They naturally blend into the landscape, which makes them difficult to spot. However, once you point out your first gator, you'll be surprised at how many are in the area. The most popular place for viewing alligators is Rookery Road. You'll know you are in the right place if you see stopped cars. This is one of the few swamps accessible by car. It is recommended to bring binoculars and a camera for spotting wildlife.

Best Time to Visit: Lake Martin is open and accessible year-round.

Pass/Permit/Fees: It is free to visit the lake, but any tours or events may cost money.

Closest City or Town: Lafayette

Address: 1209 Rookery Rd., Breaux Bridge, LA 70517

GPS Coordinates: 30.2208° N, 91.9111° W

Did You Know? Lake Martin has a legend that the McIlhenny Family tried to use nutria to make fur, but the rodents escaped the factory during a hurricane and now live on the lake.

St. Martin de Tours Catholic Church

St. Martin de Tours Catholic Church is the third oldest Catholic church in Louisiana. The church was built over 250 years ago. St. Martin is comprised of two buildings, plus the church and the presbytery, or rectory, which has been the center for community events for the past two hundred years.

The church was founded in 1765 and set up by Acadian refugees. After much legislation, the church was incorporated in 1814, and the current building was built.

When visiting the grounds, you will see a monument next to the church that commemorates the people of St. Martinville who served in the Battle of Baton Rouge. The monument was the creation of the Daughters of the Revolution.

Best Time to Visit: St. Martin de Tours is open and accessible year-round except during mass and private wedding ceremonies.

Pass/Permit/Fees: It is free to visit St. Martin de Tours Catholic Church.

Closest City or Town: Lafayette

Address: 133 S. Main St., St. Martinville, LA 70582

GPS Coordinates: 30.722° N, 91.4941° W

Did You Know? St. Martin de Tours Catholic Church is one of the oldest Catholic churches in the United States.

Vermilionville

Vermilionville is located in the heart of Lafayette. It is a cultural center for all things Louisiana, Creole, Southern, Acadian, and people of African descent. Founded by an exiled person with a rich Creole cultural history, the area boasts some of the best cuisine in all of Louisiana. Vermilionville also hosts several events that celebrate the history of Louisiana with music, cooking, and conservation. One of the missions of the site is to connect Louisiana's past with its present. When you visit Vermilionville, you can take guided tours through the village. You can access and see historic buildings that have been around for centuries, as well as attend music concerts, rent canoes, and kayaks, and shop Native American, Acadian, and Creole crafts. There is a venue to hold weddings in Vermilionville, and it is photographers' go-to place for photos of traditional Louisiana.

Best Time to Visit: Vermilionville is open year-round, Tuesday through Sunday. It is closed on major holidays and during Mardi Gras.

Pass/Permit/Fees: It costs $10 per adult. Children are free. There are discounted admission rates for groups.

Closest City or Town: Lafayette

Address: 300 Fisher Rd., Lafayette, LA 70508

GPS Coordinates: 30.1251° N, 91.9963° W

Did You Know? When Vermilionville was first founded, all its streets were named after presidents.

DeQuincy Railroad Museum

The DeQuincy Railroad Museum is home to exhibits revolving around the Missouri Pacific, Union Pacific, and Kansas City Southern Railroads. Located in the old railroad town of DeQuincy, most of the artifacts making up the museum were donated by local railroading families. Opened in 1974 in the 1923 Kansas City Southern Depot, the museum educates visitors and the community about the vital impact the railroad has on DeQuincy's history and lives. In the museum, visitors can expect to see a 1913 restored steam locomotive, a 1947 passenger coach, two vintage cabooses, and multiple model trains, including a collection of Gauge 1steam and diesel engines. As the town centers around the railroad, many people in the area are hobbyists and take an active role in preserving the town's history through the museum. As such, an exciting time to visit is the second weekend of April when enthusiasts gather for the Railroad Days Festival.

Best Time to Visit: The museum is open from 10 a.m. to 5 p.m., Tuesday through Saturday.

Pass/Permit/Fees: It is free to enter the museum.

Closest City or Town: Lake Charles

Address: 400 Lake Charles Ave., Dequincy, LA 70633

GPS Coordinates: 30.4518° N, 93.4350° W

Did You Know? Standardized time zones were created solely to help railroads organize an easy-to-understand schedule for the public.

Holly Beach

Holly Beach is located in the heel of the boot of Louisiana. Holly Beach has been the location of several hurricanes in the past 75 years. In 1957, Hurricane Audrey completely leveled the beach town, and then it was hit again in 2005 by Hurricane Rita. Since 2005, Holly Beach has sustained the floods and storm surges of Hurricane Ike, Hurricane Gustav, and Hurricane Laura. Despite these natural disasters, the iconic beaches still stand, and most of the town has been rebuilt.

Although it is recommended to wear water shoes and swimming is discouraged, this is still a great spot for many activities. Visitors often enjoy crabbing, fishing, and shell hunting from the beach's shores. Known for its Cajun culture, Holly Beach is romanticized in many popular songs like "(Holly Beach) Under the Boardwalk" by Kenny Tibbs, which is a spoof of the original "Under the Boardwalk," "Laisse les Bons Temps Rouler," and "La Valse de Holly Beach."

Best Time to Visit: Accessible all year long.

Pass/Permit/Fees: Holly Beach is free.

Closest City or Town: Lake Charles

Address: Hwy 82, Cameron, LA 70631

GPS Coordinates: 29.7670° N, 93.4591° W

Did You Know? Holly Beach doesn't have a modern sewer system. A lot of people use portable toilets in town.

Little Florida Beach

Located in Cameron Parish, just down the road from Holly Beach, Little Florida Beach is known as the Cajun Riviera. The beach is very quiet and secluded as it is not often marketed to tourists. There are also no markets or restaurants in the area, so bring plenty of your own food and snacks.

Swimming safety at the beach must be taken seriously as the water is consistently tested for bacteria. If the green flag is flying, that means the water is safe to use. Otherwise, swimming at a neighboring beach may be a better idea.

Although swimming is not the main attraction at this beach, many people come here because it is one of the stops on the Creole Nature Trail and All-American Byway. Hiking and shell hunting are popular activities here. This is also one of the few beaches where dogs and driving on the white sands are permitted.

Best Time to Visit: Little Florida beach is accessible year-round.

Pass/Permit/Fees: It is free to enjoy the beach.

Closest City or Town: Lake Charles

Address: 154-1762 Beach Blvd., Cameron, LA 70631

GPS Coordinates: 29.7553° N, 93.6087° W

Did You Know? There is a huge gas line pipe that sits right in the middle of the beach.

Millennium Park

Millennium Park is a family fun park located in Lake Charles on the lakefront. There is a rock-climbing wall, pirate ship, tree house, and a full playground of slides, monkey bars, and ladders.

There is a shaded area in the park for eating and picnicking with the whole family. The ground is covered in a thick, soft rubber for extra safety as kids run and play with their friends.

One of the more popular parts of Millennium Park is the splash park, where kids can come and play in the summertime in a cool environment out of the summer heat. The park is split between younger kids and older kids.

Best Time to Visit: Millennium Park is open and accessible all year long.

Pass/Permit/Fees: It is free to enjoy Millennium Park. There is a fee to reserve picnic areas or to access the beach and splash pad. It is $4 for adults and $2 for children ages 3 - 15.

Closest City or Town: Lake Charles

Address: 900 Lakeshore Dr., Lake Charles, LA 70601

GPS Coordinates: 30.2251° N, 93.2216° W

Did You Know? There was a fire in Millennium Park that closed it for some time until it was rebuilt and reopened.

North Beach

North Beach is an urban beach located off of Interstate 10 just before the Louisiana/Texas border near Lake Charles. It is a nice respite for the city dwellers nearby who come to cool off in its waters.

It is a unique beach with white sand and access to the cool waters of the lake. Visitors can use the lake for a variety of water sports, or they can take their time exploring the town of Lake Charles and all it has to offer.

You will find visitors playing volleyball, jet skiing, and sunbathing. Although the waters are murky, most people do swim in the area. Pets are officially not allowed on the beach, but often times locals will bring their dogs on a leash.

Best Time to Visit: North Beach is accessible year-round but best in the summer months.

Pass/Permit/Fees: North Beach is a public beach and is free to enter.

Closest City or Town: Lake Charles

Address: N. Lakeshore Dr., Lake Charles, LA 70601

GPS Coordinates: 30.2360° N, 93.2377° W

Did You Know? Between Florida and Texas, North Beach is the only inland beach with white sand.

Rutherford Beach

Rutherford Beach is located in Cameron Parish, just south of Creole and Oak Grove. The beach is located close to the Mermentau River. The beach offers a variety of summer and water sports activities.

You can canoe or kayak in the Gulf of Mexico or the Mermentau River. The water in that general area is shallow, so it is safe for beginners. However, it is important to remember that winds off the gulf can make paddling difficult. A lot of people like to collect seashells, swim, and paddle.

You can camp for free on the beach, and dogs are also allowed in the area. There are public grills and picnic tables for gatherings, and for campers, there are showers available for use.

Best Time to Visit: Rutherford Beach is accessible year-round.

Pass/Permit/Fees: It is free to enjoy Rutherford Beach.

Closest City or Town: Lake Charles

Address: Gulf of Mexico, Creole, LA 70632

GPS Coordinates: 29.7586° N, 93.1240° W

Did You Know? When you set up your camp on the beach, you can drive your car on the sand. Also, the nearest convenience store is 6 miles away.

Sam Houston Jones State Park

Sam Houston Jones Park is named after the forty-sixth Governor of Louisiana. With over 1,000 acres of well-maintained forest, rivers, and lakes, this state park is home to 200 species of birds. This makes it one of the most popular spots in Louisiana for birding. In addition to birds, this state park is unique because it focuses on the rehabilitation of the oldest living southern pine species in America. With over 70 acres of longleaf pine forests, visitors often enjoy traipsing through the three hiking trails throughout the park. One of the most memorable of which is an old stagecoach road that follows along a Calcasieu River tributary. Camping is welcome, and the state park has eight cabins, sixty-two campsites, and nineteen tent sites. The eight cabins come with two bedrooms, a living\dining room, a bathroom, and a fully stocked kitchen.

Best Time to Visit: Sam Houston Jones State Park is open and accessible year-round.

Pass/Permit/Fees: It costs $3 to enter the park. Children under age 3 are free, and adults 62 and older are free.

Closest City or Town: Lake Charles

Address: 107 Sutherland Rd., Lake Charles, LA 70611

GPS Coordinates: 30.1807° N, 93.1531° W

Did You Know? Sam Houston Jones was not only a governor but also recognized as a Texas folk hero who spent time exploring western Louisiana.

Lake Claiborne State Park

Founded in 1974, Lake Claiborne is a manmade lake and outdoor recreation area encompassing 643 acres of wilderness. With 6,400 square acres of water and a pristine, sandy beach, this is a popular spot for watersports and fishing. Fishermen travel from all over the state to catch catfish, black crappie, striped bass, chain pickerel, bream, white perch, and sunfish. The woods around the lake are full of wildlife and hiking trails. One of the most popular trails is the White Tail Trail. This easy six-mile loop welcomes leashed dogs. Unfortunately, the trail is poorly marked, so make sure and study the map as it is the only reliable way of navigating. Overnight camping is available. There are a total of eighty-seven campsites complete with water, electricity, picnic tables, and barbeques. There are also ten cabins, a "comfort station," and places to do laundry.

Best Time to Visit: Lake Claiborne is accessible year-round.

Pass/Permit/Fees: It costs $3 to enter the lake. Children under age 3 are free, and adults 62 and over are free. There is a cost to camp and do other activities.

Closest City or Town: Lisbon

Address: 225 State Park Rd., Homer, LA 71040

GPS Coordinates: 32.7236° N, 92.9228° W

Did You Know? Lake Claiborne is home to the top two disc golf courses in Louisiana.

Tickfaw State Park

Tickfaw State Park is known for its forest and swamp areas, including cypress-tupelo swamps, a mixed pine and hardwood forest, and a hardwood forest on the bottomland.

The land periodically floods in the winter and spring, and this water is exactly what is needed to keep the balance of the ecosystem in order.

There are vacation cabins on the property that can be rented where you can see and experience nature from your screened-in porch.

There are lots of hiking trails as well as biking. Visitors can canoe or kayak on the Tickfaw River. The park has a nature center where you can learn all about the ecosystem of the park, animals, and plant life in the area.

Best Time to Visit: Tickfaw State Park is open and accessible year-round.

Pass/Permit/Fees: It is $3 to enter the park. Children under age 3 are free, as are seniors 62 and older.

Closest City or Town: Killian

Address: 27225 Patterson Rd., Springfield, LA 70462

GPS Coordinates: 30.3845° N, 90.6507° W

Did You Know? There is an 800-gallon aquarium at the nature center where you can see fish from the Tickfaw River.

Grand Cote National Refuge

Grand Cote National Refuge is made up of 6,000 acres of land dedicated to helping preserve and protect the wildlife of Louisiana. It was created in 1989 through the North American Waterfowl Management Plan, which was established by Canada and the United States in 1986 (Mexico would join in 1994) to protect the waterfowl species of the continent. The area is perfect for waterfowl because the refuge sits in a basin that typically collects a large amount of water after rainfall. Because the area floods and water pools on the soil, the result is a nutrient-rich soil that resembles clay and can support the waterfowls' life and massive numbers. It also creates an ideal environment for growing rice, which attracts and feeds northern pintails. Most visitors enjoy taking the Dupuy Wildlife Trail, which is an easy 1.1 loop. The trail leads to a lookout over the refuge and is landscaped enough for stroller use. Visitors can expect to see waterfowl and deer in this area.

Best Time to Visit: Grand Cote National Wildlife Refuge is open and accessible all year long.

Pass/Permit/Fees: It is free to enjoy the refuge.

Closest City or Town: Marksville

Address: 401 Island Rd., Marksville, LA 71351

GPS Coordinates: 31.0630° N, 92.0815° W

Did You Know? At one point in history, the land was cleared to be a farm.

New Orleans

New Orleans is one of the most famous cities in the world. It is the home of Mardi Gras, or Fat Tuesday, which is the day before Ash Wednesday and marks the final party before Lent.

New Orleans is named after Philippe II, Duke of Orleans, when the French occupied Louisiana. Today, New Orleans is a commercial hub for commerce and shipping from the Gulf of Mexico as it sits on the Mississippi River.

Aside from award-winning Cajun cuisine, New Orleans is the jazz capital of the world, where some of the greatest jazz musicians of all time have played and resided. The famous Bourbon Street is in New Orleans, which is full of bars and restaurants and is the epicenter for partying.

Best Time to Visit: Accessible year-round, New Orleans is best in the winter when it's not hurricane season and it's Mardi Gras season.

Pass/Permit/Fees: It is free to enjoy New Orleans, although you will need to factor in the cost for outings.

Closest City or Town: Metairie

Address: New Orleans, LA 70130

GPS Coordinates: 29.5738° N, 90.4175° W

Did You Know? New Orleans is actually below sea level. It sits in a basin area below the water line, and the city is protected from flooding by levees.

Chemin-A-Haut State Park

Chemin-A-Haut State Park is located on a cliff above Bayou Bartholomew. Chemin-A-Haut State Park has two playgrounds and a wading pool for younger children. There is also a swimming pool for older kids and adults open in the summer months from Memorial Day to Labor Day.

An RV park is available for camping as well as traditional campgrounds. For those who would like to spend the night, there are cabins to rent, some of which are private and located on the bayou.

In the park, you will find Big Slough Lake. It is located near the shore and offers freshwater fishing with many species for catching.

Best Time to Visit: Chemin-A-Haut is accessible year-round between the hours of 6 a.m. and 10 p.m.

Pass/Permit/Fees: It costs $3 to enter the park. Children under age 3 and seniors 62 and older are free.

Closest City or Town: Monroe

Address: 14656 State Park Rd., Bastrop, LA 71220

GPS Coordinates: 32.9089° N, 91.8492° W

Did You Know? This state park gets its name from a French word that means "high road." The park was part of a route that was used by Native Americans as they traveled around the Gulf region during the year.

Jimmie Davis State Park

Jimmie Davis State Park is located on the Caney Creek Reservoir in north-central Louisiana on a peninsula. There are boat launches on the lake as well as freshwater fishing. The most popular activity is waterskiing as the lake water is crystal clear.

The lake is surrounded by a hardwood and pine forest. The park also has biking trails for cyclists, playgrounds for kids, and plenty of spots for bird watchers.

Immie Davis State Park has 73 camping sites offering accommodations for both RVs and tents. In addition to camping, there are seventeen cabins and two lodges with a central dining hall.

Best Time to Visit: Accessible year-round between the hours of 6 a.m. and 10 p.m.

Pass/Permit/Fees: It costs $3 to enter. Children under age 3 and seniors over 62 are free.

Closest City or Town: Monroe

Address: 1209 State Park Rd., Chatham, LA 71226

GPS Coordinates: 32.2585° N, 92.5182° W

Did You Know? The park opened in 1996 as Caney Creek Lake State Park. The name was changed to Jimmie Davis State Park in 2003 after Louisiana governor Jimmie Davis, who served from 1944 - 1948 and again from 1960 - 1964.

Ouachita River

The Ouachita River is 605 miles long. It begins in Arkansas and flows south into Louisiana. It ends at the Tensas River, where both bodies of water form the Black River in Jonesville, Louisiana.

Eventually, the river joins other rivers that flow in the Atchafalaya River to the Mississippi River to the Gulf of Mexico. The river is named after the Ouachita Tribe of Native Americans that once inhabited the land that is today's Ouachita River.

Historians believe the word Ouachita (owa chitto) is a Choctaw phrase that means "hunt big." Other tribes that dwelled along the river were Choctaws, Osage, Chickasaw, and Caddo.

Best Time to Visit: Ouachita River can be accessed anytime.

Pass/Permit/Fees: It is free to see the river.

Closest City or Town: Monroe

Address: Jonesville, LA 71343

GPS Coordinates: 31.6312° N, 91.8070° W

Did You Know? The Ouachita River is the twenty-fifth longest river in the United States.

Venice

Located on the very tip of the boot of Louisiana, Venice is a small town of a few hundred people. Venice has an extremely diverse variety of fish, which makes it one of the best and most popular places to fish in all of Louisiana. It is located where the Gulf of Mexico meets the Mississippi River, so fishermen can get a mixture of freshwater and saltwater fish. The town can be found at the end of Great River Road, and it is the last town in Louisiana you can reach by automobile. Due to its location, Venice has a history of being impacted by natural disasters. In 1969, the entire community was almost completely wiped out by Category 5 Hurricane Camille and again in 2005 by Category 3 Hurricane Katrina. Most recently, in 2021, Venice was also affected by Category 4 Hurricane Ida. In 2010, Venice was almost the center of an environmental disaster when the Deepwater Horizon exploded, and oil began to wash ashore on the beaches.

Best Time to Visit: Venice is accessible year-round, but it is safest when it is not hurricane season.

Pass/Permit/Fees: It is free to enter Venice.

Closest City or Town: Myrtle Grove

Address: Boothville-Venice, LA 70091

GPS Coordinates: 29.1637° N, 89.2117° W

Did You Know? Venice is located at the very end of Louisiana, which is why it has the nickname "The End of the World."

Cane River National Heritage Area

Cane River National Heritage Area is a place dedicated to the preservation and promotion of the culture of the Cane River Region. They hold a fall festival every October and also host plays that depict life in the South from the Revolution War through the Civil War and into the twentieth century. Hiking trails and wildlife refuges, lakes, and forests compliment this rich historical site and provide a diverse array of activities for visitors.

No Man's Land was an area that used to exist near the Cane River. There was no government or leader because it was a zone between the United States and Spanish Texas. While this zone didn't belong to either country, it was home to bandits, outlaws, pirates, and pioneers.

Best Time to Visit: Cane River National Heritage Area is open year-round. Some attractions are not open on the weekends.

Pass/Permit/Fees: It is free to enjoy the heritage area.

Closest City or Town: Natchitoches

Address: 4115 University Pkwy., Natchitoches, LA 71457

GPS Coordinates: 31.7698° N, 93.0856° W

Did You Know? Colonial forts, plantations, churches, and cemeteries come together to preserve over 300-years of history in the Cane River National Heritage Area.

Melrose Plantation

Melrose Plantation is located in the north-central part of Louisiana in Natchitoches Parish. The plantation is one of the largest in the United States. It is remarkable in that it is one of the biggest plantations in America built by and for freed slaves. The house was built in 1832, and the Metoyer Family ran the property.

Today, Melrose Plantation is a museum with artifacts from its plantation era, and there are also tours through the grounds. You can either take a guided tour or a self-guided tour. There are nine buildings on the grounds that you can visit, including a gift shop. The plantation also hosts seasonal festivals and is home to a collection of art by famous African American folk artist Clementine Hunter.

Best Time to Visit: Melrose Plantation is open Thursday through Monday. It is closed Tuesday, Wednesday, and all major holidays.

Pass/Permit/Fees: Guided tours cost $15 per person, and self-guided tours cost $5.

Closest City or Town: Natchitoches

Address: 3533 LA-119, Melrose, LA 71452

GPS Coordinates: 31.3559° N, 92.5800° W

Did You Know? The Metoyer family, who built the plantation, was free for four generations before the onset of the Civil War.

Avery Island / Avery Island Bird Sanctuary

Avery Island is a salt dome located in Iberia Parish, just a few miles north of Vermilion Bay. The bay is an opening to the Gulf of Mexico. A salt dome is a massive mound of sand, and Avery Island is surrounded by marshland, making it an island. Native Americans who lived on the island used to mine salt and sell it to other tribes and settlers for money and food. On the island is the Avery Island Bird Sanctuary. It's referred to as Bird City, and it is a refuge for wildfowl. It was founded by Edward Avery McIlhenny, who noticed the absence of the snowy egret. McIlhenny traveled around the Gulf Coast until he found some egret birds and set them free in his refuge. Theodore Roosevelt once heralded Bird City as "the most noteworthy refuge in the country."

Best Time to Visit: Avery Island and Bird City are accessible year-round.

Pass/Permit/Fees: Entry to Bird City costs $8 for adults and $5 for children.

Closest City or Town: New Iberia

Address: Louisiana 329 and Main Rd., Avery Island, LA 70513

GPS Coordinates: 29.8968° N, 91.9050° W

Did You Know? The McIlhenny family purchased and lived on Avery Island. The McIlhenny family is famous for being the creators and proprietors of Tabasco Sauce.

Cypremort Point Beach

Cypremort Point Beach is a man-made beach in Cypremort Point State Park. It is popular with visitors who want to come and relax for the day. You can picnic, fish, waterski, windsurf, sail, and crab from this area. There is a direct connection to the Gulf of Mexico and Vermilion Bay, so if you want to access the boat launch, you can go out into the gulf or the bay and fish for redfish and flounder.

There is a fish cleaning station on the dock near the boat launch where you can have your catch cleaned and filleted for you. For nature lovers, there are plenty of areas to walk around and see the wildlife. The beach area has black bears, rabbits, foxes, muskrats, alligators, and nutria. The area consists of about 185 acres of marshland.

Best Time to Visit: Cypremort Point Beach is open and accessible year-round, but it is considered best to visit in the summer months.

Pass/Permit/Fees: It costs $3 to enter the beach, but children under age 3 are free, as are seniors ages 62 and older.

Closest City or Town: New Iberia

Address: 306 Beach Ln., Cypremort Point, LA 70538

GPS Coordinates: 29.7374° N, 91.8546° W

Did You Know? Cypremort Point Beach is one of the few areas along Louisiana's Gulf Coast that can be accessed by car.

Jungle Gardens

Jungle Gardens is a wildlife reserve and preservation site on Avery Island run by the McIlhenny family, who are the creators and operators of Tabasco Sauce. McIlhenny had a passion for nature and did all he could to preserve it. There are a few attractions in Jungle Gardens that many people love to come and enjoy. There is Bird City, which is a rookery that began in 1911 when McIlhenny wanted to save the snowy egret. Within 16 years, hundreds of thousands of different birds sought refuge in Bird City.

Other sites to see are a refuge for animals, including black bears, cats, otters, muskrats, armadillos, and coyotes. You can also see a bamboo forest that McIlhenny started with help from the USDA. McIlhenny's opinions on bamboo and how it helps the environment are still followed by scientists today.

Best Time to Visit: Jungle Gardens is open all year long.

Pass/Permit/Fees: Self-guided tours cost $8 for adults and $5 for children ages 5 and older.

Closest City or Town: New Iberia

Address: Louisiana 329 and Main Rd., Avery Island, LA 70513

GPS Coordinates: 29.9129° N, 91.9063° W

Did You Know? There is a Buddha statue on the grounds. It is believed to be hundreds of years old. People come from all around to pray near the statue.

Lake Fausse Pointe State Park

Lake Fausse State Park is 6,000 acres of open land located in the Atchafalaya Basin in southeast Louisiana. The area was occupied by Native Americans until the mid-1700s. Despite the Spanish governing the area from 1763 to 1802, most of the Euroamerican settlers were French and Acadian farmers and trappers.

The lake is popular for outdoor activities. There are both hiking and canoe trails throughout the park. A boat launch makes it a popular spot for fishermen. The park welcomes overnight guests. There are both lake-front cabins as well as "rough" camping sites. Once visitors have finished exploring the Lake Fausse wilderness, there are a plethora of culturally significant attractions, including the city of St. Martinville and Longfellow-Evangeline State Historic Site.

Best Time to Visit: Lake Fausse Pointe State Park is accessible year-round.

Pass/Permit/Fees: It costs $3 to enter the park. Children under age 3 and adults 62 and over are free. There are additional fees for camping and other activities.

Closest City or Town: New Iberia

Address: 5400 Levee Rd., St. Martinville, LA 70582

GPS Coordinates: 30.0588° N, 91.6045° W

Did You Know? The natural owners of the Lake Fausse Pointe State Park were the Chitimacha Tribe.

American Italian Museum

The American Italian Museum is located in the American Italian Cultural Center in New Orleans. The cultural center's mission is to celebrate and pay honor to the Italian heritage of Louisiana. The cultural center offers Italian classes, concerts, and various events that show how Italian culture played a role in shaping and inspiring local government and traditions in Louisiana.

The museum portion of the center chronicles the Italian immigrant experience from the choices that led to the departure of the home country of Italy to the journey one took to the New World arriving in New York City. The museum also tells the tales of those arriving immigrants who made the choice to move south and eventually settle in Louisiana and how they affected the city's history and development.

Best Time to Visit: The museum is open Monday through Saturday.

Pass/Permit/Fees: Guided tours are $20 for adults and $10 for students and seniors. Self-guided tours are $10 for adults and $7 for students and seniors.

Closest City or Town: New Orleans

Address: 537 S. Peters St., New Orleans, LA 70130

GPS Coordinates: 29.9476° N, 90.0661° W

Did You Know? The museum also has a sports hall of fame for famous Italian athletes.

Audubon Aquarium of the Americas

Audubon Aquarium of the Americas is located in New Orleans, in the French Quarter neighborhood. The aquarium is located on the Mississippi River and has over 10,000 animals that cover about 530 species. The aquarium depicts marine life in North and South America.

There are four major areas of the Americas that the aquarium focuses on, including the Caribbean, with a 30-foot-long tunnel that houses Caribbean fish.

There is an exhibit on the Amazon that has a greenhouse that is home to animals like anacondas and piranhas. The Mississippi River exhibit has alligators, owls, and catfish. The Gulf of Mexico exhibit has sea turtles and sharks.

Best Time to Visit: The aquarium is open Thursday through Monday. It is closed on Tuesday and Wednesday.

Pass/Permit/Fees: Tickets for adults cost $29.95, and children's tickets cost $24.95. Reservations are recommended.

Closest City or Town: New Orleans

Address: 1 Canal St., New Orleans, LA 70130

GPS Coordinates: 29.571° N, 90.347° W

Did You Know? When Hurricane Katrina flooded New Orleans, the aquarium lost power, and almost 10,000 fish died.

Audubon Park

Audubon Park is a park in the Uptown neighborhood of New Orleans, just to the west of the center of the city. Audubon Park rests on the Mississippi River, and it is relatively close to Tulane University and Loyola University. The park has fountains, walkways, open spaces, and a golf course. The golf course is named after David Berger, an athlete of Tulane University who was captured and killed during the Olympic hostage crisis in 1972.

There is a variety of wildlife in the park and a rookery for egrets and herons as well as other bird species. There are black-bellied whistling ducks in the park's lagoons. Visitors can take advantage of the picnic area along the Mississippi River for small gatherings. Audubon Zoo is located in the park, which was once the host of the World's Fair.

Best Time to Visit: Audubon Park is open all year long.

Pass/Permit/Fees: It is free to enjoy the park, but some attractions may cost a fee.

Closest City or Town: New Orleans

Address: 6500 Magazine St., New Orleans, LA 70118

GPS Coordinates: 29.5603° N, 90.0725° W

Did You Know? Audubon Park is named after John James Audubon, a naturalist, and artist, who lived in New Orleans in 1821.

Barataria Preserve

As part of the Jean Lafitte National Historical Park, Barataria Preserve is a nature preserve for Louisiana's wildlife and wetlands. You can take guided tours through the wetlands and see the vegetation, trees, and animals up close. There are alligators, otters, herons, egrets, and a variety of other animals on the preserve, including turtles. There are over 200 species of birds, and blooming wildflowers change throughout the year.

While in the preserve, there are also trails for hiking as well as canoeing and kayaking. The Old Barataria Trail is a popular 4.3-mile loop. Although the trail is heavily trafficked, it is overgrown, and fallen trees sometimes cross the path. Prepare for mud as you wander down this palmetto-dense excursion.

Best Time to Visit: Barataria Preserve is open and accessible year-round, but the parking lot closes at 5 p.m. daily. The park itself is closed on Monday and Tuesday and all major holidays.

Pass/Permit/Fees: It is free to enter the preserve.

Closest City or Town: New Orleans

Address: 6588 Barataria Blvd., Marrero, LA 70072

GPS Coordinates: 29.7839° N, 90.1155° W

Did You Know? Barataria is part of the Jean Lafitte Historical Park, making it one of the most important cultural areas of Louisiana.

Bayou Sauvage National Wildlife Refuge

Bayou Sauvage National Wildlife Refuge is located in Eastern New Orleans in a place called Lacombe. It is the largest urban wildlife refuge in the United States.

To protect the refuge, it is surrounded by hurricane levees since most of the land is below sea level. The refuge is made up of natural bayous, marshlands, and brackish marshes.

There are over 340 different species of birds at any given time of the year, and it is also home to shrimp, fish, and crabs. The brown pelican can be found at the refuge as well as white pelicans, alligators, marsh rabbits, and raptors.

Best Time to Visit: The refuge is open year-round, but it is only open during daylight hours.

Pass/Permit/Fees: It is free to enter the Bayou Sauvage National Wildlife Refuge.

Closest City or Town: New Orleans

Address: 61389 LA-434, Lacombe, LA 70445

GPS Coordinates: 30.3219° N, 89.9355° W

Did You Know? Bayou Sauvage was originally going to be a planned community. Three exits were built off the highway to access the development. Two were never used, and they are ghost exits off of Interstate 10.

Bourbon Street

One of the most famous streets in the world, Bourbon Street is home to the yearly Mardi Gras celebration. Bourbon Street is in the heart of the French Quarter, the oldest neighborhood in New Orleans. This street shows off its French influence with architecture of wrought iron balconies and pastel colors. Bourbon Street is also the center for jazz musicians who come from all over the world to play on the famous thoroughfare. It stretches from Esplanade Avenue to Canal Street and is lined with bars and restaurants that serve the best Creole-influenced foods in the world. It is also legal to have open containers of alcohol on the street, so you will see many patrons walking from establishment to establishment having fun with friends while eating and drinking.

Best Time to Visit: Bourbon Street is open all year long but is at its most vibrant during Mardi Gras.

Pass/Permit/Fees: It's free to visit Bourbon Street, but all bars, restaurants, and other attractions will cost money.

Closest City or Town: New Orleans

Address: Bourbon St., New Orleans, LA 70116

GPS Coordinates: 29.9592° N, 90.0650° W

Did You Know? Bourbon Street is not named for the alcohol. Bourbon was the surname of a French royal family.

Caesars Superdome

Caesars Superdome is home to the New Orleans Saints. It is also home to other sporting events. The Sugar Bowl, one of college football's bowl games, has been played at the Superdome since 1975. The men's NCAA basketball tournament has also been played in the dome as well as the "Bayou Classic," which is a rivalry game between Grambling State University and HBCUs Southern University. The Superdome has also hosted seven Super Bowls for the NFL, with the eighth Super Bowl being hosted in 2025. One of the biggest historical markers for the Superdome was in 2005 when it was used as a shelter for New Orleans residents during Hurricane Katrina. The dome was subsequently closed and refurbished for the opening of the New Orleans Saints football season in 2006. It has been previously known as the Louisiana Superdome and the Mercedes-Benz Superdome.

Best Time to Visit: The Caesars Superdome is open and accessible all year long.

Pass/Permit/Fees: It is free to enter the Superdome, but to see any shows or any sporting events will require the purchase of a ticket.

Closest City or Town: New Orleans, Louisiana

Address: 1500 Sugar Bowl Dr., New Orleans, LA 70112

GPS Coordinates: 29.573° N, 90.452° W

Did You Know? Caesars Superdome is the largest domed structure in the world. It covers 13 acres, and its dome has a diameter of 680 feet.

Carousel Gardens

Carousel Gardens is an amusement park in New Orleans. The 1300-acre park has attracted guests since 1850. The park features a mini-train as well as a drop tower, Ferris wheel, and a rollercoaster called the Live Oak Ladybug.

There are other rides for kids and adults to enjoy, like the famous carousel from which the park gets its name. The carousel in the amusement park has been operating for more than 100 years.

It has the nickname "The Flying Horses," and the carousel still runs on its original motor from 1906. It is the only handcrafted carousel left in the state of Louisiana and one of a hundred left in the United States.

Best Time to Visit: Carousel Gardens is only open on Saturday and Sunday.

Pass/Permit/Fees: $25 per person, $13 for senior citizens. Any child under three feet tall may enter for free.

Closest City or Town: New Orleans

Address: 7 Victory Ave., New Orleans, LA 70124

GPS Coordinates: 29.9872° N, 90.0991° W

Did You Know? The amusement park is located in New Orleans' City Park, giving visitors access to other attractions like City Put and Story Land.

Confederate Memorial Museum

The Confederate Memorial Museum tells the story of the Confederate Army and the rise of the Confederacy in the mid-1800s that brought on the American Civil War.

The museum opened in January of 1891, just thirty-six years after the end of the Civil War. The museum is filled with artifacts, including weapons that were used in battles, as well as the uniforms that were worn by Confederate soldiers.

One exhibit is about the Red River Campaign, where thousands of soldiers led by Richard Taylor and Jefferson Davis were defeated by the Union Army. You will see weapons, flags, and other items from that campaign.

Best Time to Visit: The Confederate Museum is open Tuesday through Saturday.

Pass/Permit/Fees: Adult entry is $10, and children ages 7 to 14 years old pay $5.

Closest City or Town: New Orleans

Address: 2336 Esplanade Ave., New Orleans, LA 70119

GPS Coordinates: 29.9433° N, 90.0713° W

Did You Know? The Confederate Memorial Museum is the oldest museum in Louisiana, and it is the largest collection of Confederate artifacts in the United States.

Contemporary Arts Center

Established in 1976, the Contemporary Arts Center was the brainchild of a collection of artists who wanted to preserve and help foster visual and performing arts in New Orleans. The center hosts classes in various art disciplines. In addition to the art on display and lessons available, the arts center hosts live theater, dance, concerts, lectures, and special events. Current event calendars are available on the Contemporary Arts Center website.

It is the center's belief that art should be accessible by everyone no matter their background, and everyone should have the opportunity to see live and visual performances as a means of being further educated and exposed to art in a meaningful way. The center has 10,000 square feet of space for teaching and performance.

Best Time to Visit: The center is open and accessible all year long. The gallery is closed on Tuesdays.

Pass/Permit/Fees: To access the gallery, tickets are $10 for adults and $8 for students and seniors.

Closest City or Town: New Orleans

Address: 900 Camp St., New Orleans, LA 70130

GPS Coordinates: 29.9437° N, 90.0728° W

Did You Know? The Arts Center teaches and involves about 10,000 children and adults every year of various socio-economic backgrounds, including children and adults with special needs.

Elms Mansion

Elms Mansion is a historic mansion located in New Orleans. The house was built in 1869 and was originally built for Watson Van Benthuysen. He was nicknamed the "Yankee in Gray" because he was born in New York. When the Civil War started, he sided with the Confederate Army and was an officer. He was in Richmond when the Confederate presidential convoy fled the city. He became president of the Saint Charles Streetcar Company after the war and died in 1901.

From 1931 to the beginnings of WWII, the mansion was a German Consulate where the Consul General informed U-Boats in the Gulf of Mexico of the departure of ships from New Orleans. In the 1950s, the house was purchased by John Elms. After his death, the family began to use the house as an event venue, and today it is still a premier place to hold weddings.

Best Time to Visit: Elms Mansion is open all year long.

Pass/Permit/Fees: Tours are available by request, and all fees are discussed at the time of your request.

Closest City or Town: New Orleans

Address: 3029 St. Charles Ave., New Orleans, LA 70115

GPS Coordinates: 29.5546° N, 90.0520° W

Did You Know? The original owner, Watson Van Benthuysen, was related to Jefferson Davis through marriage.

Fair Grounds Race Course

Located in New Orleans, the Fair Grounds Race Course is the third oldest location for horse racing in the United States. It was first established in 1838, and horses have been running there ever since. When it first opened, the races lasted five days before the track closed. It reopened again from 1852 - 1857.

After a brief closure, it reopened in 1872. In the 1940s, when horse racing was officially legal in Louisiana, the grounds were going to be demolished, but a group of people stepped in and saved the track; and after WWII, racing resumed.

Throughout the twentieth century, there were more hardships for the track as hurricanes and fires caused closures and rebuilding several times. Today, Fair Grounds boasts slot machine casinos, dining, and entertainment.

Best Time to Visit: The Fair Grounds Race Course is open and accessible all year long.

Pass/Permit/Fees: It is free to enter, but activities like gambling and dining cost money.

Closest City or Town: New Orleans

Address: 1751 Gentilly Blvd., New Orleans, LA 70119

GPS Coordinates: 29.5855° N, 90.4418° W

Did You Know? The racetrack is operated by Churchill Downs, the same group that operates the Kentucky Derby.

French Quarter

The French Quarter is a section of New Orleans that is reminiscent of the city's French heritage. The French Quarter is located downtown and is the home of New Orleans' jazz and party scenes. The buildings of the French Quarter are colorful, and they have a distinct architecture of wrought-iron balconies. This is the location of Bourbon Street, and at the onset of Lent, the day before Ash Wednesday, the infamous Mardi Gras, or Fat Tuesday, celebration.

There are quieter streets in the French Quarter that are quaint and filled with shopping and dining. The French market offers crafts and gourmet foods. Another famous part of the French Quarter is Jackson Square, where you will find St. Louis Cathedral. Street performers can be found there performing for large crowds.

Best Time to Visit: The French Quarter is most vibrant during Mardi Gras.

Pass/Permit/Fees: It is free to walk around the French Quarter.

Closest City or Town: New Orleans

Address: French Quarter, New Orleans, LA 70130

GPS Coordinates: 29.5718° N, 90.0332° W

Did You Know? The French Quarter is known as "Vieux Carre" because it is the oldest neighborhood in New Orleans.

Fontainebleau State Park

Named after a famous forest near Paris, Fontainebleau State Park sits on the shore of Lake Pontchartrain, and it offers a beach for sunbathers and swimmers.

The 2,800-acre park was once home to Bernard de Marigny de Mandeville's sugar plantation in 1852. He named the plantation after a forest located in Paris, France, which was a frequent recreation spot for kings.

There was once a railroad that went through the park, but it has since been converted to an area that skaters, bikers, runners, and walkers can use to exercise and enjoy the beauty of the park. Throughout the trail, you'll find signs to help you identify trees and animals that live in the area. People who want to stay overnight can rent cabins that are right on the edge of the lake.

Best Time to Visit: Fontainebleau State Park is open and accessible year-round.

Pass/Permit/Fees: It costs $3 to enter the park. Children under age 3 are free, as are seniors 62 and older.

Closest City or Town: New Orleans

Address: 62883 LA-1089, Mandeville, LA 70448

GPS Coordinates: 30.3376° N, 90.0381° W

Did You Know? There are ruins of an old 1829 sugar mill in the park that was built by Marigny de Mandeville.

Honey Island Swamp

Honey Island Swamp offers tours of the swamp area just north of New Orleans on the other side of Lake Pontchartrain. You can have private tours or group tours in covered or uncovered boats for varying prices. The swamp is home to alligators, pelicans, marsh plants, and it gets its name from the honeybee. Honey Island is located between East Pearl and West Pearl Rivers.

You may also see deer, wolves, and several species of exotic birds. The area is a popular spot for fishing. People who fish here have been known to catch buffalo fish, catfish, and alligator gar. Several thousand pounds of crawfish are caught in the waters each year.

Best Time to Visit: Honey Island Swamp is open and accessible year-round.

Pass/Permit/Fees: To take tours of the swamp, there is a price range depending on what tour you choose. Ticket prices range from $25 - $54 for adults and $15 - $32 for children.

Closest City or Town: New Orleans

Address: 41490 Crawford Landing Rd., Slidell, LA 70461

GPS Coordinates: 30.3025° N, 89.7072° W

Did You Know? Honey Island Swamp is virtually untouched. It's still in its original condition and has never been altered.

House of Broel's Victorian Mansion and Doll House Museum

House of Broel is an antebellum mansion that has stood for hundreds of years, but it is also a museum of dolls and dollhouses that were created by owner Bonnie Broel. It is the single largest collection of miniature art by any artist in one location. It is also a fashion museum. By appointment, guests can tour the house and the second floor that houses all the dolls and dollhouses. The second floor has hundreds of doll art as well. There are miniatures of dollhouses and vignettes of dolls "living" in their element. Bonnie Broel has even managed to make miniatures of real-life locations, like her father's farm. There is a 2,000-year-old piece of Egyptian cotton on the second floor, as well as a French desk from 1850. The Broels date back to the Russian Empire.

Best Time to Visit: House of Broel is open and accessible all year long.

Pass/Permit/Fees: Tours are by appointment only, and all fees are discussed when you book.

Closest City or Town: New Orleans

Address: 2220 St. Charles Ave., New Orleans, LA 70130

GPS Coordinates: 29.9336° N, 90.0810° W

Did You Know? Owner Bonnie Broel wrote the book *House of Broel: The Inside Story,* where she tells tales of being in the house and her noble family.

Jackson Barracks Military Museum

The Jackson Barracks Military Museum is dedicated to Louisiana history through the story of the National Guard. From the early years of French and Spanish occupation through the Confederacy and to modern times in terms of natural disasters, the National Guard has played a major role in Louisiana's history.

On display in the museum are uniforms, machine guns, and additional exhibits about women who helped serve in the military. There are artifacts about the path Louisiana took to become a state. You will also see exhibits about WWI, WWII, and the Persian Gulf War.

Best Time to Visit: The museum is open and accessible all year long. It is closed on Sundays.

Pass/Permit/Fees: It is free to enjoy the Louisiana National Guard Museum at Jackson Barracks.

Closest City or Town: New Orleans

Address: 4209 Chenault Blvd., New Orleans, LA 70117

GPS Coordinates: 29.9580° N, 90.0065° W

Did You Know? William Cousans was the pharmacist in the barracks during the Civil War. He got the job because he was a Confederate supporter who was captured by the Union Army and his punishment was to help cure the Union soldiers who had taken over the barracks.

Jackson Square

Jackson Square is an open space in the French Quarter neighborhood of New Orleans. Jackson Square is most famous for the number of buskers and performance artists who put on shows for visitors and passersby. The square is also home to St. Louis Catholic Cathedral. The park is located on Decatur Street.

While in the square, you will see the famous equestrian statue of Andrew Jackson, who won the Battle of Orleans and was the seventh president of the United States. Most of the park is designed to look like a Parisian park, and that architecture and style are still intact today, lasting since its inception in 1851. The park is a historic landmark, and among its historical elements, you can see a fountain named after Charles de Gaulle.

Best Time to Visit: Jackson Square is open and accessible all year long.

Pass/Permit/Fees: It is free to enjoy Jackson Square.

Closest City or Town: New Orleans

Address: 701 Decatur St., New Orleans, LA 70116

GPS Coordinates: 29.5725° N, 90.3470° W

Did You Know? Jackson Square was the location in 1803 when Louisiana was made a United States territory in the deal of the Louisiana Purchase.

Jean Lafitte National Historic Park and Preserve

Jean Lafitte National Historic Park and Preserve is a cultural spot in southern Louisiana. The park's mission is to preserve the history and culture of Louisiana's southernmost points. The park and preserve are broken up into six different areas, each one preserving a different part of Louisiana's history.

Barataria Preserve is 23,000 acres of preserved wetlands in Marrero, Louisiana. There are several animals to see in the preserve, including turtles, reptiles, birds, and alligators. The other areas of the park are scattered around southern Louisiana, and they depict the culture and heritage of the Cajun people, the cemetery and battleground of the War of 1812, and prairie life.

Best Time to Visit: The Barataria preserve is open year-round except during Mardi Gras.

Pass/Permit/Fees: It is free to enjoy all areas of Jean Lafitte Park. The centers do accept donations.

Closest City or Town: For the wetlands area, the closest city is New Orleans.

Address: Marrero, LA 70072

GPS Coordinates: 29.8472° N, 90.1496° W

Did You Know? Jean Lafitte was a French pirate who used to steal from merchant ships. He helped the Americans win the Battle of New Orleans during the War of 1812.

Lafayette Cemetery No.1

Lafayette Cemetery No. 1, built in 1833, gets its name from its original location, Lafayette. Lafayette (not the current city of Lafayette) was a suburb that eventually joined the city of New Orleans, though the cemetery retained its name. The cemetery is still active today, and it was designed for mausoleums and tombs because the southern heat and potential for flooding caused Louisianans to put their loved ones to rest above ground.

Lafayette Cemetery No. 1 is located in the Garden District of New Orleans. In 1995, novelist Ann Rice, who writes many novels based in New Orleans, emerged from a coffin after being carried through the cemetery to promote her new book. The cemetery has also been mentioned in other novels, and it has been the location for several music videos and movies.

Best Time to Visit: Lafayette Cemetery No. 1 is accessible all year long; however, it may be closed on occasion for renovations.

Pass/Permit/Fees: It is free to walk through the cemetery, but guided tours, when available, cost $5.40.

Closest City or Town: New Orleans

Address: 1427 Washington Ave., New Orleans, LA 70130

GPS Coordinates: 29.9288° N, 90.0854° W

Did You Know? Lafayette Cemetery No. 1 is the final resting place for about 7,000 people.

Lafayette Cemetery No. 2

Lafayette Cemetery No. 2 is the sister cemetery to Lafayette Cemetery No.1 and No. 3. Just like the other two sites, this particular area of New Orleans was once known as the town of Lafayette. When Lafayette joined New Orleans, the cemeteries kept their names. All of the graves are above ground in a mausoleum-style layout because flooding and extreme heat are not conducive to keeping human remains underground. Lafayette Cemetery No. 2 is the final resting place for those who were part of the African American Labors Society as well as the Butchers Society. The cemetery is located in the Garden District of New Orleans, just up the street from Lafayette Cemetery No. 1 and next to St. Joseph's Cemetery. Many of the mausoleums had to be refurbished because the bodies have been there so long that family members are no longer associated with the individual to keep up their final resting place.

Best Time to Visit: The cemetery is open and accessible all year long.

Pass/Permit/Fees: It is free to enter the cemetery.

Closest City or Town: New Orleans

Address: 2110 Washington Ave., New Orleans, LA 70113

GPS Coordinates: 29.9355° N, 90.0895° W

Did You Know? Lafayette Cemetery No. 2 is mostly dedicated to those who served in the labor movement in New Orleans.

Lake Maurepas

Lake Maurepas is located just to the west of Lake Pontchartrain. It is just about the halfway point between New Orleans and Baton Rouge, a tidal estuary that receives freshwater from four different sources. Water enters the lake from the Tickfaw River, the Blind River, the Natalbany River, and the Amite River.

The lake is also connected to Lake Pontchartrain via the Pass Manchac. Lake Maurepas is large at more than 15,000 acres of water, but by fishing standards, it's small. There are really no towns, developments, or any kind of industry near the lake.

Lake Maurepas was named after the eighteenth-century statesman, Jean-Frédéric Phélypeaux comte of Maurepas. Phélypeaux was chief adviser to King Louis XVI and the son of Louis Phélypeaux comte de Pontchartrain which is who Lake Pontchartrain was named after.

Best Time to Visit: Lake Maurepas is accessible year-round.

Pass/Permit/Fees: It is free to visit Lake Maurepas.

Closest City or Town: New Orleans

Address: Maurepas, LA 70449

GPS Coordinates: 30.2734° N, 90.5069° W

Did You Know? Lake Maurepas is the second largest lake in Louisiana.

Lake Pontchartrain

Lake Pontchartrain is located in the south-eastern part of Louisiana in New Orleans. The city sits on the lake and has a direct connection to the Lake Pontchartrain Causeway that connects New Orleans to Louisiana to the north. It is an estuary that borders six Louisiana parishes and offers a direct connection to the Gulf of Mexico. It is believed that Lake Pontchartrain was formed between 2,600 and 4,000 years ago when the Mississippi Delta was formed.

Lake Pontchartrain was responsible for some of the flooding during 2005's Hurricane Katrina. New Orleans sits below sea level, and there are levees that help keep the city safe from flood waters. However, the storm surge from the hurricane was too much for the levees to handle, and the city flooded after the levees broke.

Lake Pontchartrain is one of the largest wetland areas in North America, with 125,000 acres.

Best Time to Visit: Lake Pontchartrain is accessible year-round.

Pass/Permit/Fees: It is free to visit Lake Pontchartrain.

Closest City or Town: New Orleans

Address: 3939 N Causeway Blvd., Metairie, LA 70002

GPS Coordinates: 30.2051° N, 90.1121° W

Did You Know? Native Americans called Lake Pontchartrain "Okwata," which means wide water.

Laura Plantation

Laura Plantation was a sugar plantation built in 1804 on the banks of the Mississippi River just outside of New Orleans. Today, the plantation is a Creole Heritage Museum honoring the life and history of the Acadian people. The plantation was originally built by slaves of Senegalese descent. The plantation is named after Laura Locoul, who grew up on the plantation.

After Laura got married, she moved to her husband's hometown of St. Louis, Missouri. While living in St. Louis, Laura wrote memoirs titled "Memories of the Old Plantation Home," which depicted her life growing up on the plantation. The memoirs were discovered in the mid-1990s and published.

Best Time to Visit: Laura Plantation is open and accessible year-round but is closed on major holidays and during Mardi Gras.

Pass/Permit/Fees: It costs $25 for adults to enter Laura Plantation. The cost for teenagers to enter is $15, and children ages 6 - 12 must pay $10.

Closest City or Town: New Orleans

Address: 2247 LA-18, Vacherie, LA 70090

GPS Coordinates: 30.0081° N, 90.7253° W

Did You Know? Laura Plantation was originally named L'Habitation Duparc after its founder Guillaume Duparc.

Louis Armstrong Park

Louis Armstrong Park is located in New Orleans and named after Louis Armstrong, one of the greatest jazz musicians in history. It can be found in the Treme neighborhood. Upon entering the park, you will pass under an archway that will lead you to a huge statue of Louis Armstrong holding his trumpet, the instrument he was renowned for playing.

Inside the park, there are open spaces for enjoying nature and the outdoors, and you will find the Mahalia Jackson Theater. In the theater, they hold performances by the Louisiana Philharmonic Orchestra, the New Orleans Opera Association, and the New Orleans Ballet Association. Another prominent area of the park is Congo Square, which was a meeting place for slaves and freed African slaves during the nineteenth century.

Best Time to Visit: Louis Armstrong Park is open and accessible all year long.

Pass/Permit/Fees: It is free to enjoy Louis Armstrong Park, but you will need tickets for any shows in the theater.

Closest City or Town: New Orleans

Address: 701 N. Rampart St., New Orleans, LA 70116

GPS Coordinates: 29.9628° N, 90.0678° W

Did You Know? Louis Armstrong Park is within walking distance of the French Quarter, the convention center, and the Super Dome.

Louisiana Children's Museum

The Louisiana Children's Museum is located in the City Park section of New Orleans. The museum is a place where kids can come to play and learn with interactive exhibits. It is the belief of the museum that kids learn best when they are playing. The museum is 30,000 square feet of space for children and adults to enjoy.

Some of the exhibits you will see are the Sharing Station where you can use microscopes, a sedimentation table where you can build levees, a station where you can learn about caring for animals, and there is a place where you can stand inside a giant bubble. A grocery store with a real cash register is also part of the fun to teach children about food.

Best Time to Visit: The Louisiana Children's Museum is open and accessible all year long. The museum is closed on Monday and Tuesday.

Pass/Permit/Fees: It costs $14 for children and adults to enter the museum.

Closest City or Town: New Orleans

Address: 15 Henry Thomas Dr., New Orleans, LA 70124

GPS Coordinates: 29.9898° N, 90.0940° W

Did You Know? You can host birthday parties and other events for kids at the museum.

Maurepas Swamp

Maurepas Swamp is a cypress-tupelo swamp that is flooded during a large portion of the year. The floods that happen here form from eastward rains and can last for days. It is located west of New Orleans on the shore of Lake Maurepas.

The swamp is home to a variety of trees and vegetation. While there, you can see red maples, sugarberry trees, aquatic ferns, and obtusa oak. Activities include hunting and trapping, camping, birding, hiking, and fishing.

The hiking trail is about a half-mile long. For those who want to come and do some bird watching, you will see osprey and bald eagles along with wood ducks, egrets, black-bellied whistling ducks, and herons.

Best Time to Visit: Though accessible year-round, keep an eye on flooding that may cause the area to close.

Pass/Permit/Fees: It is free to visit the swamp, but all activities require a permit.

Closest City or Town: New Orleans

Address: Old U.S. 51, Laplace, LA 70068

GPS Coordinates: 30.2522° N, 90.5015° W

Did You Know? There used to be a large number of waterfowl that lived on the swamp, but new vegetation is growing, making it hard for them to live there. Most of the waterfowl have moved and relocated.

Milton H. Latter Memorial Library

The Milton H. Latter Memorial Library is located in New Orleans. The library was once a 1907-era mansion that was purchased by the Latter Family. After the death of their son, they donated the mansion to the city of New Orleans, and it was turned into a library bearing the son's name.

Milton H. Latter died in Okinawa while serving in WWII. The Latters wanted to find a way to honor the memory of their son, so they purchased the house with the intention of making it into a library.

They bought the house in the late 1940s for about $100,000 and gave the city more money to help convert it into a library that still serves the community more than seventy years later.

Best Time to Visit: The Milton H. Latter Memorial Library is closed on Sundays.

Pass/Permit/Fees: It is free to enter the library.

Closest City or Town: New Orleans

Address: 5120 St. Charles Ave., New Orleans, LA 70115

GPS Coordinates: 29.5535° N, 90.6367° W

Did You Know? Before the Latters and the Eddys, the house was owned by Marguerite Clark, one of the most famous silent movie stars of all time.

Musee Conti Wax Museum / Conti Street

Conti Street is deeply rooted in New Orleans history and folklore. The Jefferson School, an all-boys school, was opened on Conti Street, where several duels took place between the boys. Some of the boys did not survive. Other people and businesses were part of Conti Street's history, and there were fires, deaths, and lawsuits.

As a result, many feel the street is haunted with all the spirits of the dearly departed. The Musee Conti Wax Museum was present until 2016. After it closed, bones were found in the walls of the museum.

Many say they used to see ghosts in the building. The Musee Conti Wax Museum was a popular spot for tourists. The wax figures depicted history in all its forms, from historical figures to pop culture icons.

Best Time to Visit: Conti Street is open and accessible all year long.

Pass/Permit/Fees: It is free to visit Conti Street, but dining and entertainment cost a fee.

Closest City or Town: New Orleans

Address: 917 Conti St., New Orleans, LA 70112

GPS Coordinates: 29.9590° N, 90.0652° W

Did You Know? Conti Street was the site of the first black-owned and operated newspaper in New Orleans: The New Orleans Tribune.

Museum of the American Cocktail

The Museum of the American Cocktail is dedicated to the history of the cocktail in American bars and the education of mixology. The museum holds several bartending seminars and exhibits. Every year, there is an award ceremony called the Olives that takes place at the museum. Founded in 2004 by experts in mixology, spirits, and bartending, the exhibits show visitors how current pop culture and art have influenced the cocktail. There are also artifacts that you can see, such as bar tools from the time of Prohibition, as well as other tools used throughout the decades. There is also a collection of liquor bottles from the past 100 to 150 years. The museum has a publication, and it is associated with the United States Bartender Guild.

Best Time to Visit: The American Cocktail Museum is open all year long, but it is closed on Tuesday and Wednesday.

Pass/Permit/Fees: Tickets to the museum cost $10.50 per person. Children under age 12 are free when accompanied by an adult.

Closest City or Town: New Orleans

Address: 1504 Oretha Castle Haley Blvd., New Orleans, LA 70113

GPS Coordinates: 29.9409° N, 90.0791° W

Did You Know? Brunch was created in New Orleans. The museum has an exhibit dedicated to brunch, and they also host brunches that you can attend.

Museum of the Free People of Color

The Museum of the Free People of Color or Le Musee de f.p.c. is one of the only museums in America that houses material possessions, artifacts, and culture of free people of color in the United States. The museum presents this unique culture of people who were born free or set free from slavery.

By the time the Civil War began, there were over 18,000 free people of color in New Orleans who owned and paid taxes on property that was valued up to $15 million. The community produced artists and artisans as well as journalists and doctors. Most noteworthy were the politicians who came from this community and were the first to mold what would become the modern Civil Rights Movement with laws dating back to 1862.

Best Time to Visit: The museum is open and available Wednesday through Sunday. It is closed on Mondays and Tuesdays.

Pass/Permit/Fees: Tours are by appointment only, and they cost $20 per person.

Closest City or Town: New Orleans

Address: 2336 Esplanade Ave., New Orleans, LA 70119

GPS Coordinates: 29.5826° N, 90.4324° W

Did You Know? Esplanade Avenue, where the museum is located, was the location where the first free people of color purchased homes and owned land.

National WWII Museum

In New Orleans, visitors will find the National WWII Museum accounting for the battles, causes, and repercussions of the war that dramatically changed the course of history worldwide. The museum aims to instill a sense of American pride in its guests, and therefore focuses on the United States' involvement in the war. The National WWII Museum hopes to educate future generations about WWII and how it affected the nation. Throughout the museum, there are pavilions that focus on one or more of the significant battles or moments in the history of WWII in order to pay tribute to the men and women who sacrificed their lives to defeat the enemy. Visitors can also book a stay at The Higgins Hotel & Conference Center, which is located on the museum campus. History buffs will marvel at the additional information displayed throughout the hotel via artifacts, artwork, photography, and story plaques.

Best Time to Visit: The National World War II Museum is accessible year-round.

Pass/Permit/Fees: Tickets to the museum cost $29.50 for adults, $25.50 for seniors, and $18 for school-aged children.

Closest City or Town: New Orleans

Address: 945 Magazine St., New Orleans, LA 70130

GPS Coordinates: 29.5621° N, 90.0479° W

Did You Know? Congress declared the museum to be the nation's premiere museum on the subject of World War II.

New Orleans African American Museum

The New Orleans African American Museum is located in the Treme neighborhood, one of the first fully-integrated neighborhoods in the city. Treme is also the birthplace of jazz music, which has its roots in African American culture. The museum pays homage to the history of the culture with exhibits, artifacts, and historical items that tell the story from slavery to emancipation through Reconstruction and into the modern world. The museum aims to preserve all the contributions made to the history and culture of the South, including Louisiana and New Orleans, by people of color, both enslaved and free. The site was once a plantation that was purchased by the city and turned into a museum. There are rotating exhibits in the museum of current artists from the area.

Best Time to Visit: The museum is open Thursday through Sunday. It is closed Monday through Wednesday.

Pass/Permit/Fees: General Admission to the museum is $10 for adults and $5 for children under age 12. There are other tours you can choose at varying prices.

Closest City or Town: New Orleans

Address: 1418 Governor Nicholls St., New Orleans, LA 70116

GPS Coordinates: 29.9665° N, 90.0680° W

Did You Know? The Treme neighborhood of New Orleans is the oldest surviving black neighborhood in the United States.

New Orleans Museum of Art

The New Orleans Museum of Art (NOMA) is a fine arts museum in the City Park neighborhood of New Orleans. The collection of the museum spans from the Italian Renaissance to the modern era. You will find artwork ranging from Monet to Pollack. The NOMA also features Spanish art, Indian art, and works from the South Pacific, Indonesia, and Africa.

The museum also works with other smaller museums for special events and exhibits of American culture and Egyptian art. There is a sculpture garden for visitors to enjoy. The museum was originally known as the Delgado Museum of Art because it was funded by philanthropist and art aficionado Isaac Delgado. He began the museum in 1911, and it was completed in December, but Delgado couldn't attend the opening because he was sick. He died a few weeks later.

Best Time to Visit: The New Orleans Museum of Art is open all year long. It is closed on Mondays.

Pass/Permit/Fees: Adult tickets cost $15, and senior tickets are $10. Children are free.

Closest City or Town: New Orleans

Address: 1 Collins Diboll Cir., New Orleans, LA 70124

GPS Coordinates: 29.9864° N, 90.0934° W

Did You Know? The New Orleans Museum of Art is the oldest fine arts museum in New Orleans.

New Orleans Pharmacy Museum

The New Orleans Pharmacy Museum is located in the Vieux Carre Historic District. It is one of the oldest apothecary shops in New Orleans. The museum is dedicated to educating the public about the history of pharmacy in the United States. There was a long period of time when pharmacies were not regulated, and just about anyone could apprentice at a pharmacy for six months and then start making their own medicine without any kind of test or training. The museum chronicles those dark times, and there are several exhibits on display. On the first floor, you can see Voodoo medicine, the first surgical tools, opium, cosmetics, and perfumes. On the second floor, there is a showcase of eyeglasses, a sick room, and a physician's study. The building is a Historic Landmark, being one of the first apothecaries.

Best Time to Visit: The New Orleans Pharmacy Museum is open and accessible all year. It is closed Sunday, Monday, and Tuesday.

Pass/Permit/Fees: It costs $5 for adults to enter and $4 for children.

Closest City or Town: New Orleans

Address: 514 Chartres St., New Orleans, LA 70130

GPS Coordinates: 29.5721° N, 90.3536° W

Did You Know? Louis J. Dufilho, Jr. owned the apothecary. His pharmacy was the first accredited institution of its kind in the United States.

New Orleans Tattoo Museum

The New Orleans Tattoo Museum is located in the Good Words Tattoo Parlor on St. Claude Avenue in the Bywater. The museum is dedicated to the history of tattooing and celebrates the artists of tattooing in New Orleans. It houses several artifacts and information about the history of the tattoo. While you are there, you will see original tattooing tools used by the early tattoo artists of the area, including needles and portable batteries.

You will also get to see photos of early tattooing and what was popular during certain periods, along with an inside glimpse into the culture that was prominent at the time. There is an exhibit to "Doc" Don Lucas, who was a tattoo historian who lived in New Orleans. The museum is always accepting artifacts and historically accurate information about tattooing.

Best Time to Visit: The tattoo museum is open and accessible all year long.

Pass/Permit/Fees: It is free to enjoy the tattoo museum.

Closest City or Town: New Orleans

Address: 1915 Martin Luther King Jr Blvd., New Orleans, LA 70113

GPS Coordinates: 29.9655° N, 90.0359° W

Did You Know? One of the ways the museum is supported is by visitors getting tattoos. You can walk in and get a tattoo done in the tattoo parlor.

Ogden Museum of Southern Art

The Ogden Museum of Southern Art is located in the Warehouse Arts District of New Orleans. There are two buildings that make up the museum, which are the Patrick F. Taylor Library and Stephen Goldring Hall. The latter is a five-story building that houses some of the best southern art in the United States. The collections in the museum cover fifteen southern states and Washington, D.C. You can see art from Virginia and West Virginia, Texas, Tennessee, North and South Carolina, Oklahoma, Mississippi, Maryland, Kentucky, Florida, Georgia, Alabama, Arkansas, and Louisiana. There are paintings and photography of the bayous and depictions of Southern life. The main themes of the museum are history and memories.

Best Time to Visit: Ogden Museum is open and accessible all year long except on major holidays.

Pass/Permit/Fees: Tickets for adults are $13.50, and children ages 5 to 17 are $6.75.

Closest City or Town: New Orleans

Address: 925 Camp St., New Orleans, LA 70130

GPS Coordinates: 29.9437° N, 90.0714° W

Did You Know? The museum is located in the same area as the National World War II Museum and the New Orleans Contemporary Arts Center. All three centers serve about 11 million visitors a year and are affiliates of the Smithsonian.

Our Lady of Guadalupe Catholic Church

Our Lady of Guadalupe Church is located in New Orleans next to Lafayette Cemetery No. 1. The church was a mortuary chapel during the yellow fever outbreak in 1827. The church was purposely built next to the cemetery. St. Anthony's had to be built because it was believed that dead bodies could still spread the disease, so parishioners had another location to worship.

During the 1930s, many residents began to pray to St. Jude, and most found their prayers were answered. Before long, people began to come from all around to pray to St. Jude at Our Lady of Guadalupe.

Due to the popularity of the saint, a shrine was built to him to the left of the altar. The shrine is still in use today as people still come to pray to St. Jude. Novenas are still said to St. Jude at the church.

Best Time to Visit: Our Lady of Guadalupe is open and accessible all year long except during certain events.

Pass/Permit/Fees: It is free to visit.

Closest City or Town: New Orleans

Address: 411 N. Rampart St., New Orleans, LA 70112

GPS Coordinates: 29.5730° N, 90.4147° W

Did You Know? In the church, you will find a statue of Saint Expedite, which is worshipped by Catholics and those who practice Voodoo. Both beliefs pray side by side.

Port Pontchartrain Lighthouse

Port Pontchartrain Lighthouse is located in New Orleans on Lake Pontchartrain. It was originally called the Milneburg Lighthouse. The lighthouse was part of the resort town of Milneburg that used to serve the residents of New Orleans. There was a railroad built between the French Quarter and Milneburg so that visitors could cool off at the lake during the hot summer months. Originally, the lighthouse was supposed to be 18 feet high, but the railroad asked for the lighthouse to be elevated so that it was easier for them to locate their destination in the dark. The government took over and allotted a certain amount of money to build the structure. Once built, the structure rose to twenty-eight feet high. A new lighthouse was built in the 1850s, which stands today.

Best Time to Visit: The lighthouse can be visited all year long.

Pass/Permit/Fees: It is free to visit the lighthouse.

Closest City or Town: New Orleans

Address: 8001 Lakeshore Dr., New Orleans, LA 70148

GPS Coordinates: 30.1372° N, 90.4433° W

Did You Know? Alexander Milne, who owned the land that the lighthouse is built on, came to the New World because he didn't want to wear a wig over his red hair as was the law in his native Scotland.

St. Mary's Assumption

St. Mary's Assumption Church is a historic landmark in the Garden District of New Orleans. The church was built in 1860 due to the growing German-Catholic population that was moving to the neighborhood.

There is a shrine in the church dedicated to Father Francis Xavier Seelos. Father Seelos came to the United States from Germany in the 1860s to be a priest and leader at St. Mary's for the population who only spoke German.

A few years later, there was a yellow fever outbreak, and Father Seelos was on the front lines helping those who were sick. In 1867, he contracted yellow fever and died. A shrine was built for him inside the church, and in 2000 the Catholic Church beatified Father Seelos for his efforts in the 1860s.

Best Time to Visit: The church is open and available all year long.

Pass/Permit/Fees: It is free to enter St. Mary's Assumption.

Closest City or Town: New Orleans

Address: 923 Josephine St., New Orleans, LA 70130

GPS Coordinates: 29.5544° N, 90.4290° W

Did You Know? Across the street from St. Mary's is St. Alphonsus Church, which was built at the same time to help the growing Irish Catholic population.

Sydney and Walda Besthoff Sculpture Garden

The Sydney and Walda Besthoff Sculpture Garden is part of the New Orleans Art Museum. There are over ninety works of art in the garden that are of various heights and textures. Some of the art was created and cast in the 1960s, while other pieces are from the 21st century.

There are pathways and water fixtures throughout the grounds as you walk along and take in the art. Some of the pathways are art pieces themselves, like Elyn Zimmerman's "Mississippi Meanders," which is a colorful bridge.

The garden is located just next to the New Orleans Art Museum and covers about 11 acres of the park. The sculptures are surrounded by magnolias, pines, oak, and two lagoons.

Best Time to Visit: The sculpture garden is open and accessible all year long.

Pass/Permit/Fees: It is free to enter the garden. Donations are accepted.

Closest City or Town: New Orleans

Address: 1 Collins Diboll Cir., New Orleans, LA 70124

GPS Coordinates: 29.9859° N, 90.0940° W

Did You Know? The museum opened in 2003, but by 2019 had doubled in size to its current acreage.

Royal Street

Royal Street, located in the French Quarter neighborhood of New Orleans, is most famous for its antique shops, hotels, and art galleries. The street runs from Canal Street through several neighborhoods. It is interrupted by the Industrial Canal and multiple parks to end at Community Street at the Jackson Barracks.

It is known to be affluent because of the various high-end shops that are located on the street. While in the French Quarter, there are three blocks of Royal Street that are closed off to make a pedestrian walkway that is filled with street performers.

Most of Royal Street is protected against flooding because it runs through the French Quarter. The French Quarter is the original New Orleans neighborhood, and it is built on naturally high ground.

Best Time to Visit: Royal Street is open and accessible all year long.

Pass/Permit/Fees: It is free to enjoy Royal Street.

Closest City or Town: New Orleans

Address: Royal St., New Orleans, LA 70116

GPS Coordinates: 29.9643° N, 90.0495° W

Did You Know? The 700 blocks of Royal Street are home to the galleries of New Orleans-based artists Georges Rodrigue and Ally Burguieres.

Seven Sisters Oak

The Seven Sisters Oak is a live oak tree that stands 68-feet tall and has a circumference of 39 feet. The limbs stretch over 153 feet, making this tree a behemoth amongst its peers. It is believed the tree is about 500 to 1200 years old. The tree is the president of the Live Oak Society, a collection of America's most prestigious oak trees, and gets its name from Mrs. Carole Hendry Doby, who first sponsored the tree into the society. Because Mrs. Doby was one of seven sisters, the society nicknamed the tree Seven Sisters. Unfortunately, the tree is protected on private property. However, visitors are able to see the ancient being from the roadside. It is recommended to look up images of the tree before visiting, so you can easily spot the Seven Sisters Oak amongst the other beautiful oaks in the area.

Best Time to Visit: The tree is on private property and cannot be viewed by the public.

Pass/Permit/Fees: There is no public admittance to see the tree.

Closest City or Town: New Orleans

Address: Exact home and location are private.

GPS Coordinates: 30.2211° N, 90.0533° W

Did You Know? There was much dispute over whether or not Seven Sisters was one tree or many that grew together. In 1976, a team of experts surveyed the tree and determined that it was born from a single root system.

St. Elizabeth's Orphanage Museum

St. Elizabeth's has experienced a colorful history. The building was erected and opened in 1865, right after the Civil War. It was originally a school for the neighborhood children. However, the mission of education only lasted five years before the building was converted into an orphanage. The orphanage was for girls only, and as time went on, it became known as St. Elizabeth's Home for Girls. The home closed in 1989. In 1993, it was converted into a residence for about ten years, and then in 2005, it was sold to a developer who turned the building into condominiums, which is how the building remains. Visitors can expect to tour the beautiful structure. Of Italian design, the three-story building houses twenty-eight flats with high ceilings, wood floors, exposed brick walls concealed behind oversized doors, remaining true to the 1860s architecture that makes this museum stunning.

Best Time to Visit: St. Elizabeth's is accessible all year long.

Pass/Permit/Fees: It is free to visit St. Elizabeth's Orphanage building.

Closest City or Town: New Orleans

Address: 1314 Napoleon Ave., New Orleans, LA 70115

GPS Coordinates: 29.9246° N, 90.1023° W

Did You Know? The building was purchased by famous novelist Ann Rice, who converted the building into her home and showroom in 1993 before selling it.

St. Louis Cathedral

The full name of St. Louis Cathedral is Cathedral-Basilica of Saint Louis, King of France. It is located in the French Quarter neighborhood of New Orleans, and it is right next to Jackson Square, where you will see buskers and performers putting on shows for people who visit the area.

The Cathedral is believed to be haunted by Father Antonio de Sedella, who is buried within the church. They say he walks through an alley that is named after him, and he can be seen by the altar on Christmas morning. Friar Pere Dagobert, who once lived in the church, is said to haunt the Cathedral as well, chanting on rainy days.

Best Time to Visit: St. Louis Cathedral is open and accessible all year long.

Pass/Permit/Fees: For self-guided tours, the brochure is a $1 donation. Self-guided tours of the historic convent are $8.

Closest City or Town: New Orleans

Address: 615 Pere Antoine Alley, New Orleans, LA 70116

GPS Coordinates: 29.9580° N, 90.0637° W

Did You Know? In 1909, a dynamite bomb went off inside the Cathedral, damaging most of the interior. A few years later, the foundation collapsed, and the church had to be closed for a year for repairs.

The New Canal Lighthouse

The New Canal Lighthouse can be found at the entrance to the New Basin Canal on Lake Pontchartrain. The building sits on a jetty that extends into the lake. The lighthouse has been rebuilt quite often during its history. It was originally built in 1838, and during its first 100 years, it was renovated or rebuilt about eight times. After a 1910 hurricane, it was moved from its original location to where it is located today.

The lighthouse was on stilts, and after 1936 concrete was placed underneath it to keep it sturdy. From the 1960s until 2001, it was a station for the Coast Guard. Today, the lighthouse is a museum where people can learn about the building's history, and it has become an environmental source for learning about the ecology and history of the lake and surrounding area.

Best Time to Visit: The lighthouse is open and accessible all year long. It is closed on Sundays and Mondays.

Pass/Permit/Fees: The entry fee for adults is $7.50 and $3 for children ages 6-12.

Closest City or Town: New Orleans

Address: 8001 Lakeshore Dr., New Orleans, LA 70124

GPS Coordinates: 30.1376° N, 90.6475° W

Did You Know? The New Basin Canal was once much larger and connected Lake Pontchartrain to what is now the New Orleans business district. It was filled in around 1950.

The Terrebonne Basin

Now an abandoned delta complex, Terrebonne Basin sits on the Gulf of Mexico in the southernmost part of Louisiana. It is a region that is separated from the mainland by a variety of lakes, bays, and swamps. Off the coast of the basin are barrier islands. The Terrebonne has been going through many ecological changes over the years. The ecosystem has been affected by the laying of gas and oil lines.

Outside of the natural wonders of the Terrebonne Basin, there are many things for visitors to do while in the area. The parish hosts a two-week-long Cajun Mardi Gras Festival each year, and many of the surrounding towns are home to museums and old plantations accounting for the parish's rich Cajun history.

Best Time to Visit: The Terrebonne Basin is open and accessible year-round.

Pass/Permit/Fees: It is free to visit the Terrebonne Basin.

Closest City or Town: New Orleans

Address: Houma, LA 70360

GPS Coordinates: 29.2300° N, 90.7533° W

Did You Know? The basin is home to 155,000 acres of swamp and 574,000 acres of marsh. The area is slowly converting to an estuary.

Treme's Petit Jazz Museum

Treme's Petit Jazz Museum is dedicated to the many years of jazz music and the people who have brought jazz to the world. The museum was started by Al Jackson, who grew up in the Treme neighborhood of New Orleans and decided to dedicate part of his life to researching and learning about jazz history.

The museum has artifacts and displays about the legends and influencers who shaped jazz music since its creation in 1895. The Treme neighborhood of New Orleans is the oldest integrated neighborhood in the city, and it has always been rich in Creole and African American culture. The neighborhood is also famous for brass bands and Mardi Gras Indians.

Best Time to Visit: Treme's Petit Jazz Museum is open Wednesday through Saturday. It is closed Sunday through Tuesday.

Pass/Permit/Fees: General Admission is $15, and children between ages 10 and 13 are $8.00. Reservations are recommended.

Closest City or Town: New Orleans

Address: 1500 Governor Nicholls St., New Orleans, LA 70116

GPS Coordinates: 29.5808° N, 90.4579° W

Did You Know? Jazz was born in the Treme neighborhood.

Voodoo Spiritual Temple

The Voodoo Spiritual Temple opened in 1990 in New Orleans. The purpose of the temple is to help all people reach their full spiritual potential. Voodoo is a West African religion that uses herbs and rituals to help believers connect to their divine destiny. The temple is led by Priestess Miriam, who believes that Voodoo is the power of the mind that reaches enlightenment through various activities.

Voodoo is one of the oldest religions in the world. At the temple, other world religions are welcome. Voodoo has long been believed to be aligned with Satanism, which is not true, and one of the missions of the temple is to dispel this misconception so that people can come to Voodoo with an open mind and learn about its practices.

Best Time to Visit: The Voodoo Spiritual Temple is open and accessible all year long.

Pass/Permit/Fees: It is free to enjoy the Voodoo Spiritual Temple although, donations are welcome.

Closest City or Town: New Orleans

Address: 1428 N. Rampart St., New Orleans, LA 70116

GPS Coordinates: 29.9661° N, 90.0630° W

Did You Know? The museum is by Congo Square Park, where slaves from Africa would practice Voodoo magic on Sundays in the eighteenth and nineteenth centuries.

Woldenberg Riverfront Park

Woldenberg Riverfront Park is located in the French Quarter neighborhood of the city, and it was once the site of warehouses. In the late 1980s, the site was cleared away, and a park was built for all to enjoy. The park extends from the Aquarium of the Americas by Canal Street and extends to Jackson Square. During the French Quarter Music Festival, the park is host to live performances.

There are several large sculptures in the park. One is a massive memorial to Holocaust victims and survivors. The sculpture is multi-faceted and shows many depictions of Jewish survival, including a Menorah and Star of David. The other sculptures that can be found in the park are dedicated to the memories of immigrants who came to Louisiana to start a new life and a large steel sculpture titled "Ocean Song."

Best Time to Visit: Woldenberg is open and accessible all year long.

Pass/Permit/Fees: It is free to enjoy.

Closest City or Town: New Orleans

Address: 1 Canal St., New Orleans, LA 70130

GPS Coordinates: 29.9573° N, 90.0611° W

Did You Know? Woldenberg Riverfront Park is named after Malcolm Woldenberg, who was a philanthropist that helped fund the construction of the park.

Caddo Lake

Caddo Lake is located on the border between Louisiana and Texas and contains 25,400 acres of wetlands. It is internationally protected under the Ramsar Convention. The lake is home to one of the largest flooded cypress forests in America. It is also the second-largest lake in the south and is the only non-oxbow natural lake in Texas. Caddo gets its name from the Caddo Tribe of Native Americans that lived on the land in western Louisiana until the nineteenth century.

The lake offers fishing, hiking, and camping in the area, but it is not fit for swimming because of the abundance of alligators that live in the water. There is tent camping as well as RV sites and cabin rentals. The RV parks are complete with full hookups.

Best Time to Visit: Caddo Lake is accessible year-round.

Pass/Permit/Fees: It costs $4 to enjoy Lake Caddo for people ages 13 and up.

Closest City or Town: Shreveport

Address: 11425 Hwy 1 North, Oil City, LA 71082

GPS Coordinates: 32.7104° N, 94.0185° W

Did You Know? Caddo Lake is the largest freshwater lake in the South.

Caddo Parish Confederate Monument

The Caddo Parish Confederate Monument is a monument to the Confederacy and the Confederate Army. It stands in front of the Caddo Parish Courthouse. It was erected by the Daughters of the Confederacy in 1905.

The top of the monument depicts a Confederate soldier while the base has busts of P.G.T. Beauregard, Henry Watkins Allen, Stonewall Jackson, and Robert E. Lee. In 2017, the Daughters of the Confederacy were asked to have the monument removed since the Confederacy stood for preserving slavery and systemic racism.

After many years of legal battles and after the events of the murder of George Floyd, the Daughters of the Confederacy agreed to have the monument moved to private land where a Civil War battle took place.

Best Time to Visit: The monument is on display all year long.

Pass/Permit/Fees: It is free to view the monument.

Closest City or Town: Shreveport

Address: 501 Texas St., Shreveport, LA 71101

GPS Coordinates: 32.3043° N, 93.4459° W

Did You Know? The monument is older than the courthouse. The courthouse wasn't built until the 1920s.

Driskill Mountain

Located near college towns in northern Louisiana, Driskill is less of a mountain and more of a hill. Its highest elevation is only 535 feet above sea level, which is shorter than many of New Orleans's skyscrapers. Due to its location and relative ease, it is a popular spot for local hikers. The Driskill Mountain Trail is a 1.8-mile hike that is rather popular, so expect crowds. Dog companions are permitted to join their owners on this trek. It is good to keep in mind that the trail winds through hardwood forests and is prone to getting muddy after rain.

The hike takes visitors past a small church and cemetery. Mount Zion Presbyterian Church and Driskill Memorial Cemetery were founded by the mountain's namesake, James Christopher Driskill, on June 26, 1883. Driskill bought 324 acres, including the mountain, and moved his wife and nine children to the area from Georgia in 1859.

Best Time to Visit: Driskill Mountain is accessible year-round.

Pass/Permit/Fees: It is free to enjoy Driskill Mountain.

Closest City or Town: Shreveport

Address: Bienville Parish

GPS Coordinates: 32.4246° N, 92.88974° W

Did You Know? Driskill Mountain is so small that it would take fifty-five of them to match the height of Mount Everest.

114

Gardens of the American Rose Center

The Gardens at the American Rose Center is home to the American Rose Society. The area is 118 acres of land that is full of roses of every kind and color. The original headquarters of the center used to be in Columbus, Ohio, before moving south.

Throughout the garden, there are sculptures and fountains, including the Dudley Watkins Reflection Pool. There are also walking and jogging trails, a children's garden, and a picnic area.

The American Rose Society has been around for 125 years with members from all over the world. It is the largest society dedicated to one single plant in all the United States. It has been in Shreveport, Louisiana, for fifty years.

Best Time to Visit: The center is open and accessible all year long.

Pass/Permit/Fees: Guided cart tours cost $10 per person.

Closest City or Town: Shreveport

Address: 8877 Jefferson Paige Rd., Shreveport, LA 71119

GPS Coordinates: 32.4598° N, 93.9494° W

Did You Know? The Gardens at the American Rose Center is the largest park dedicated to roses in the United States.

Louisiana State Exhibit Museum

The Louisiana State Exhibit Museum was opened in 1939. It was created in the modern architecture of the time, and today is a work of art in itself. The museum is the home to twenty-three dioramas that depict life in Louisiana in the 1940s. The museum's collection goes beyond life in Louisiana, and there are regional artifacts and objects that show the life of Native Americans as well as natural history and work by local artists.

For history buffs, there are artifacts from the Civil War, which include transcripts of official papers from the time. There are science exhibits on the salt domes of Louisiana, as well as an entire collection on the insects of the region. There are details about the Battle of Orleans, and the dioramas depict the harvesting practices of early farmers.

Best Time to Visit: The museum is open Monday through Friday.

Pass/Permit/Fees: It is free to enjoy the museum.

Closest City or Town: Shreveport

Address: 3015 Greenwood Rd., Shreveport, LA 71109

GPS Coordinates: 32.4803° N, 93.7853° W

Did You Know? The museum was part of the New Deal's Public works projects. It was a project that helped employ men and women who were desperately seeking work during the Great Depression.

Sci-Port Discovery Center

Sci-Port Discovery Center is a science center and museum in Shreveport. The center's mission is to introduce and help educate people of all ages in the fields of mathematics, science, and technology. There are several exhibits on site that allow visitors to have a hands-on experience in learning about nature, space, and the world. The center has several theaters for learning. There are films about sea life and the creatures of the deep. The planetarium on site also offers presentations and movies. One of the more popular exhibits is the Peggy and Aaron Selber Space Walk, which is a 15-foot tunnel that replicates outer space and allows visitors to feel as if they are walking among the stars. The PoP (Power of Play) Museum is designed to entertain children up to second grade, where they can play in an adult world.

Best Time to Visit: The center is open year-round. It is closed on Monday and Tuesday.

Pass/Permit/Fees: General admission is $15 for visitors ages 12 and older. There are other fees for some of the exhibits and the theatre.

Closest City or Town: Shreveport

Address: 820 Clyde Fant Pkwy., Shreveport, LA 71101

GPS Coordinates: 32.5134° N, 93.7420° W

Did You Know? The Sci-Port Discovery Center offers educational classes in science, math, and technology, including gaming.

Shreveport Aquarium

The Shreveport Aquarium houses about 3,000 different animals across several species. There are seven galleries in the building that you can visit and see fish and sea creatures. There is a shipwreck gallery where you can view clownfish and the WOW gallery where you can see angelfish and reef fish.

There are also classes you can take while at the aquarium to learn about coral, sharks, stingrays, and seahorses. Other animals that you can see while you are there are starfish, jellyfish, spider crabs, and moon jellies. You can host major events at the aquarium, including birthday parties and weddings.

Best Time to Visit: The Shreveport Aquarium is open and accessible all year long, seven days a week.

Pass/Permit/Fees: Visitors ages 13 and older pay $15. Visitors ages 2 - 12 pay $12. Children under age 2 enter for free.

Closest City or Town: Shreveport

Address: 601 Clyde Fant Pkwy., Shreveport, LA 71101

GPS Coordinates: 32.5159° N, 93.7433° W

Did You Know? The aquarium has a mining sluice. You can dig for treasures, gems, fossils, and gold while you are there.

Butler Greenwood Plantation

Butler Greenwood Plantation consists of 44 acres of land in St. Francisville. It is registered as an American historic place. The plantation was built and started in the 1770s by Dr. Samuel Flower, a Quaker physician from Pennsylvania. At the time, the land was controlled by the British, but when Spain took control, Dr. Flower was the physician for the Governor, Manuel Gayoso.

When Dr. Flower died, one year after Louisiana became a state, his heirs inherited the plantation where they worked it for many generations to come raising cotton, tobacco, sugar cane, and indigo. Today, the plantation is a bed and breakfast where you can stay overnight or come for the day and take tours. The house is still in its grand Victorian style with oil paintings and a grand piano.

Best Time to Visit: Butler Greenwood Plantation is open and accessible all year long.

Pass/Permit/Fees: Reservations for the cottages cost various prices determining on what room you book.

Closest City or Town: St. Francisville

Address: 8345 US-61, St. Francisville, LA 70775

GPS Coordinates: 30.8201° N, 91.3903° W

Did You Know? The same family still owns the plantation. The current occupant is the author Anne Butler. The kitchen is original from the 1790s, and the gazebo is original from the 1850s.

Lake Bruin State Park

Lake Bruin State Park is 3,000 acres of water that is very popular with water sports enthusiasts like jet skiers, water skiers, and swimmers. As a freshwater lake, there is an abundance of fishing with three large piers available. For bass fishing, the best time of year is April, May, June, September, and October.

There is also white perch and bluegill fishing, the latter of which is most popular in the shallow waters. For children, there is a water playground for splashing around with a bathhouse nearby. A large day area for picnicking offers barbecues and playgrounds near the edge of the lake.

Best Time to Visit: Lake Bruin State Park is accessible year-round.

Pass/Permit/Fees: It costs $3 for adults. Children under age 3 and adults over 62 are free. There is a cost to camp and do other activities.

Closest City or Town: St. Joseph

Address: 201 State Park Rd., St. Joseph, LA 71366

GPS Coordinates: 31.9604° N, 91.2012° W

Did You Know? Lake Bruin was originally founded in 1928 as a fish hatchery. Hatcheries help maintain the number of fish in the water, and some fish are specifically hatched for fishing and game.

Oak Alley Plantation

Oak Alley Plantation is located in Vacherie on the east bank of the Mississippi River. The plantation was originally known as Bon Sejour and was built in 1837-39. Its current name is derived from one of its most prominent features – an 800-foot double row of massive oaks. The plantation was initially owned by a French Creole, Valcour Aime, who was known as the "King of Sugar." He swapped plantations with his brother-in-law, Jacques Roman, who built the massive mansion that currently sits on the property. Today, Oak Alley Plantation is a historic landmark where you can take tours of the mansion, stay in the cottages, and walk the grounds.

Best Time to Visit: Oak Alley Plantation is open year-round except on major holidays and Mardi Gras.

Pass/Permit/Fees: It costs $27 per adult to take a tour of the mansion and the grounds, $17.50 for teenagers and older kids, and $24.50 for seniors. There are cheaper tickets available if you just want to tour the grounds but not the main house.

Closest City or Town: Thibodaux

Address: 3645 LA-18, Vacherie, LA 70090

GPS Coordinates: 30.0015° N, 90.4633° W

Did You Know? A man named Antoine lived on the grounds as a slave. He was an expert grafter and grafted pecan trees to make a pecan with a paper-thin shell. It went on to win a prize at an expo in Philadelphia.

North Toledo Bend State Park

North Toledo Bend State Park is found surrounding the banks of Toledo Bend Reservoir, which is one of the largest man-made reservoirs in the nation. With over 1200 miles of shoreline, the reservoir is a favorite for fishermen. There is a boat launch on the lake as well as a fish cleaning station for when you return with your catch. The park hosts several freshwater fishing competitions.

On land, the park encompasses more than 900 acres and contains two hiking trails. There is an easy 1.5-mile hiking loop, and for more advanced hikers, there is a 4-mile hike. There are a total of sixty-three campsites complete with water and electric hookups. There are also ten cabin rentals that can sleep up to eight each, as well as five dormitories for larger groups. Guests can enjoy a full-sized swimming pool, laundry facility, and public restrooms.

Best Time to Visit: North Toledo Bend State Park is open and accessible year-round.

Pass/Permit/Fees: It costs $3 to enter the park. Children under age 3 and adults 62 and over are free.

Closest City or Town: Zwolle

Address: 2907 N. Toledo Park Rd., Zwolle, LA 71486

GPS Coordinates: 31.3253° N, 93.4359° W

Did You Know? Toledo Bend Reservoir is one of the largest man-made reservoirs in the country.

Proper Planning

With this guide, you are well on your way to properly planning a marvelous adventure. When you plan your travels, you should become familiar with the area, save any maps to your phone for access without internet, and bring plenty of water—especially during the summer months. Depending on which adventure you choose, you will also want to bring snacks or even a lunch. For younger children, you should do your research and find destinations that best suit your family's needs. You should also plan when and where to get gas, local lodgings, and food. We've done our best to group these destinations based on nearby towns and cities to help make planning easier.

Dangerous Wildlife

There are several dangerous animals and insects you may encounter while hiking. With a good dose of caution and awareness, you can explore safely. Here are steps you can take to keep yourself and your loved ones safe from dangerous flora and fauna while exploring:

- Keep to the established trails.
- Do not look under rocks, leaves, or sticks.
- Keep hands and feet out of small crawl spaces, bushes, covered areas, or crevices.
- Wear long sleeves and pants to keep arms and legs protected.
- Keep your distance should you encounter any dangerous wildlife or plants.

Limited Cell Service

Do not rely on cell service for navigation or emergencies. Always have a map with you and let someone know where you are and how long you intend to be gone, just in case.

First Aid Information

Always travel with a first aid kit in case of emergencies.

Here are items you should be certain to include in your primary first aid kit:

- Nitrile gloves
- Blister care products
- Band-Aids in multiple sizes and waterproof type
- Ace wrap and athletic tape
- Alcohol wipes and antibiotic ointment
- Irrigation syringe
- Tweezers, nail clippers, trauma shears, safety pins
- Small zip-lock bags containing contaminated trash

It is recommended to also keep a secondary first aid kit, especially when hiking, for more serious injuries or medical emergencies. Items in this should include:

- Blood clotting sponges
- Sterile gauze pads
- Trauma pads

- Second-skin/burn treatment
- Triangular bandages/sling
- Butterfly strips
- Tincture of benzoin
- Medications (ibuprofen, acetaminophen, antihistamine, aspirin, etc.)
- Thermometer
- CPR mask
- Wilderness medicine handbook
- Antivenin

There is much more to explore, but this is a great start.

For information on all national parks, visit https://www.nps.gov/index.htm .

This site will give you information on up-to-date entrance fees and how to purchase a park pass for unlimited access to national and state parks. This site will also introduce you to all of the trails at each park.

Always check before you travel to destinations to make sure there are no closures. Some hiking trails close when there is heavy rain or snow in the area and other parks close parts of their land for the migration of wildlife. Attractions may change their hours or temporarily shut down for various reasons. Check the websites for the most up-to-date information.

Printed in Great Britain
by Amazon